HEALING THE KARMIC WOUNDS

Pluto and Chiron

BY
ALICE LOFFREDO

INKWATER
PRESS

PORTLAND • OREGON
INKWATERPRESS.COM

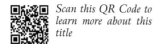
Scan this QR Code to learn more about this title

Publisher: Inkwater Press | www.inkwaterpress.com

ISBN-13 978-1-62901-539-2 | ISBN-10 1-62901-539-3

1 3 5 7 9 10 8 6 4 2

For all those who walk wounded with me.

"Content with an ordinary life you can show all people the way back to their own true nature."

...and my personal mission statement as an astrologer

ACKNOWLEDGEMENTS

FOR THE THIRD TIME I TRY TO EXPRESS THE EXTENT OF MY GRATITUDE TO those who have supported my life and its work, and found that words can only begin to do the job. But words are what I have – and love – so to the many who cheer me along my way, I offer my heartfelt thanks:

TO FAMILY AND FRIENDS AND CLIENTS AND STUDENTS.

I cannot list you all by name, for fear of omitting even a single one. Just know that I have received from you all much more than I have ever been able to give or share. Still, some names simply must be named:

- My daughters Sasha and Nikki, and my granddaughter, Lulu. I hope you know how I feel, because I can't begin to describe it.

- My sister Claudia, who's shared all but three years of this life with me and has always been in my corner.

- My niece Amanda, who shared her great talent and made my words look as good as they possibly could.

- Helen, my very own Book Angel and friend. I simply couldn't get it done without your help.

- The core review team, who took their time to read all or part of this book again and again and did so much to shape the final version: Helen, Claudia, Sasha, Nikki, and Don.

- J. (Rebecca in these pages) who told me her story and allowed me to share it with you.

- The clients: One of the gifts of this work is to meet the best people. Some of their stories enrich this book. All have enriched my life and work.

TO THE ASTROLOGERS AND TEACHERS AND GUIDES AND GURUS.

As always, I play the role of middle-man, taking the wisdom, ideas, and insights that I have been privileged to acquire from others, and translating and communicating it all to an audience that might not have happened upon it otherwise. As many of their names and works as I can remember are found in these pages and its Bibliography. Steven Forrest, a special thanks to you for your guidance, support and encouragement. Your voice is the strongest in the astro-choir that backs up my own.

And, finally, **to Don**. There are adventures we might not ever experience without the love and companionship of one special person. In my life, that person is Don, who, as he lives his own life in his very own way, enhances and enriches the unfolding of my own. More and more. Day after thankful day.

TABLE OF CONTENTS

INTRODUCTION

"Do our very wounds contain the seeds of an awakening to a state of greater wisdom, compassion, creativity and love?"

JOAN BORYSENKO
FIRE IN THE SOUL

FROM WHAT I'VE READ AND HEARD, THE IDEA OF PUBLIC SPEAKING IS one of people's greatest fears. But somehow, despite the fact that I'm inclined toward a quiet, introspective life and am actually quite shy and prefer to socialize among a small-ish number of close family and friends, I have absolutely no trouble at all getting up in front of a big audience, especially if it gives me a chance to talk about astrology. Whether it's a Barnes & Noble talk and book signing, or a speech at a women's conference, or radio interviews to publicize my latest book, it's easy – yes, easy – for me to step out and get the job done. What's more, the feedback I get suggests that I'm pretty good at it: relaxed, clear, interesting, and even amusing.

But there's another side to the coin. I look for any legitimate reason I can find *not* to pursue any item on my "To Do" list that smacks of having to initiate or follow up on a chance to take the show on the road. Eventually the window of opportunity closes and I can cross the item off the list, but never without a feeling that I've let myself – or something – down.

Until I came to understand the karmic dimension of astrology, it was a total paradoxical puzzlement. Now I get it. Every time this happens, I've just conceded another round in the life-long effort to heal my karmic wounds once and for all. Being an astrologer has given me insight into the challenge and how to meet it, for sure, but it does not offer exemption when it comes to getting the job done.

I've worked long and hard to resolve some of the gnarlier qualities of those wounds. In doing so, I've learned how wounds contain the energy needed to heal them, and claimed new-found resources that were released as a product of the healing process. I've taken authority and responsibility for setting and achieving my own life goals and have learned that it's OK to give myself what I need to sustain and nurture me in that effort. And I've reconciled important relationships. Still, delivering on the part of the mission that involves going public in a determined way to share what I have learned and experienced is still what we used to call an "opportunity area" in my long-ago corporate days. Every time I don't step up to the challenge I resolve it will be different the next time. And sometimes it is. This book is another stab at keeping that resolution.

Until I get the job done, Alice-the-Astrologer walks wounded, just like everyone else.*

* For more information about the nature of my wounds, see "*For the Record: Alice and Her Wounds*" in the Appendix.

HEALING THE KARMIC WOUNDS

CHAPTER ONE

THE WALKING WOUNDED

"Once whittled to the bone, we are faced with a never-ending choice: to become the wound or to heal."

MARK NEPO
THE BOOK OF AWAKENING

B ORN HERE ON PLANET EARTH, WE ARE ALL MEMBERS OF THE WALKING Wounded Club. A core principle of evolutionary astrology is that we are here to right what went wrong – or never got done – in the karmic past. That includes dealing with and healing wounds that we received during that past life experience. We carry them forward in our "karmic DNA," along with the history of the soul's experience during its travels through the many lifetimes of its spiritual journey.* These wounds can lock us into repetitive, hard-to-break patterns of poor decisions and behavior that erode our ability to experience and deliver on this lifetime's potentials and goals. But if we confront them consciously and work to heal them, at the end of this lifetime's day we are ready for whatever comes next, not lamenting unfinished business.

The challenge is huge because, like all of the karmic history, the wounds are buried deep in unconscious emotional memory,

---

* For a detailed explanation of how karmic history affects this lifetime's experience, there's an excerpt from my book *Perfect Together* in the Appendix, entitled "Astrology, Karma and You."

not accessible using conventional left-brained logical approaches. Not only are the wounds deep, but they are bound to hurt when we encounter them, so it's simply human nature to try to develop strong, bullet-proof defenses against letting the "monster" out of the closet. We don't do this intentionally or willfully. It's like temporary amnesia after a trauma: we do it to protect ourselves until we are ready – mature enough, strong enough, brave enough, experienced enough – to open the closet door. But there's this: if we don't face the challenge, consciously take on the intention and responsibility to heal, the wound only gets stronger and deeper, and situations that remind us of its existence get louder and more disruptive...even traumatic.

It takes great quantities of effort and energy to keep it all under lock and key, energy that would be better used to address the wounding. But experiences that "rub at the scab" and draw attention to what hurts can be scary, evoking emotional responses that leave you feeling hopeless, exhausted, sad, and in pain. And sometimes life circumstances even conspire to help you avoid the issue, like when the approval and applause you get for the commitment you have to healing the environment allows you to escape looking at the healing you need to do for yourself. To quote Steven Forrest, "If you don't open the door, you pay the storage fee until you do."

Something inside of each one of us intuitively knows that (1) we can't escape what's causing our pain, and (2) if we don't face it, we'll just be stuck in the same self-limiting, self-depleting, and self-defeating patterns forever, not only in this lifetime, but into future ones, with the patterns and pain only more intense for having become more ingrained.

So, how do you know when what you're dealing with is karmically important? It's a safe bet that when emotional suffering is way out of proportion to the situation at hand, you've probably happened upon a detonator in the karmic wound minefield. Perhaps a long-buried childhood memory of abuse or neglect stirs when you see a toddler being screamed at in the supermarket.

Childhood experiences often mirror the unfinished business and carryover wounding of the karmic past. The scene is sad and upsetting, but really not your business, yet you find yourself struggling NOT to intervene and grab the mother and scream at *her*. Instead, you abandon your groceries and run out the door, crying.

Sometimes encounters with unprocessed karmic wounding can result in physical consequences. You're rummaging for something in a long-ignored junk drawer and come upon an old photograph that brings back the memory of a romantic betrayal that occurred two relationships ago. Even though you spent eighteen months in therapy over the issue at the time, it invokes wrenching sobs, heaving shoulders, and a subsequent two-week stint with a nasty flu, despite the fact that you've had the flu shot and taken your vitamins.

However, triggering circumstances don't always have to evoke deep suffering and pain. They can resonate in a different, yet still dramatic way. Here's an example straight out of my consulting experience.

During a karmic reading several years ago I was describing a hypothetical past life story that involved the Spanish Inquisition. These stories are developed by analyzing the nature of the symbols in the birth chart and how they interconnect with each other. The themes and events that emerge are always *energetically* true, even though they may not have ever happened historically. Although my client was a woman, in that lifetime she had been male, a member of the Catholic Church hierarchy. As part of the responsibilities of his

Throughout this book I'll be mentioning past life history and we will be meeting up with characters in past life stories. It's important to know that the material applies whether or not you subscribe to the concept of reincarnation. The energetic legacy in this lifetime is real and is represented by the symbolism of your birth chart. The energies are an intrinsic part of your natal inheritance, regardless of your beliefs about how they got there.

high rank, this church official sat in judgment during the Inquisition, deciding the fate of the accused heretics that came before it. The gist of the story is that, out of the true compassion and caring that was part of his nature, he had advised and counseled those who came to him in ways that were considered to be in defiance of church law. Perhaps he condoned abstinence for a woman depleted and exhausted by poverty and the demands of her large family. Perhaps he counseled and supported escape from an abusive and violent marriage. Perhaps he had explored occult practices and used them to heal trauma. One way or another, he was found out and brought before the Inquisition as a prisoner, convicted and doomed to a dark and painful death, the kind of sentence he himself had pronounced on others.

Midway through the reading, she stopped me. "Please don't continue," she said. "I have to tell you something."

"When I was a kid we used to walk to grammar school. The shortest route took us on a block where there was a Catholic church. Being raised Presbyterian, I really didn't know much about Catholicism except that I thought that nuns were beautiful and mysterious, and I wished I could have a pretty white dress with a little veil like my Catholic girlfriends wore when they made their First Holy Communion. But here's the thing: when I walked to school I went three whole blocks out of my way to avoid that Catholic Church. I never knew why, I only knew that I got a strange, scary feeling if I passed by its doors, a feeling that made me a little sick and shaky."

"And there's something else. I can't *stand* the sound of the Spanish language," she continued. "If I'm in line at the supermarket and I hear someone having a conversation in Spanish, it's all I can do not to switch lines or even leave the store!"

The correspondences between past life stories and current life situations are rarely this dramatic or exact. But what is certainly true and has been validated time and again in my practice is that these biographies are *always* energetically true and resonate deeply with the client in some way, casting a shadow on the experiences of *this* lifetime.

Coming for the karmic reading helped this woman consciously recognize and explore situations in this lifetime that were limiting her, but whose underlying cause had been to elusive to grasp. Using the clues that emerged in the karmic reading, she was able to take up the task of healing and transformation, and at last report had been making some real progress. Her unexplainable "night terrors" are now a thing of the past. In this case, it didn't take a disproportionately upsetting event to jump-start the process. Recognizing a story that explained a heretofore inexplicable situation was enough.

No matter how you encounter it, once you're attuned to the wound, the knee-jerk reaction is most likely to call on all the defensive armament at your command so that you can calm the pain and keep life moving in a forward direction. Unless, of course, you recognize the event as an invitation to step up and examine what is going on inside, which is, of course, what would *really* keep life moving forward.

Confront the issues consciously, with courage and positive intent, and you will release the very power needed to heal. And once the healing work is done, that same energy can be used to move your life toward its full potential. And know, too, that when the time comes, you are ready to take on the task. The Universe is delivering an exquisitely synchronous invitation to roll up your sleeves and get to work. It's not likely to be easy, but it may just be easier than you think...and the effort is absolutely worth it.

ENTER ASTROLOGY

Logical, left-brained approaches don't unearth the source of karmic pain. Deep psychotherapy can touch on it, and can contribute brilliantly to healing, but getting to the source can be a slow process that may include unproductive dead-end explorations before the goal is reached. This is where astrology can come in. The symbols of the birth chart provide not only the history of our karmic past and precise explanation of the issues to be worked on, they also delineate the potentials and healing mechanisms of *this* lifetime, offering custom-designed, individualized strategies we can use to get the job done and deal with the challenges we might encounter along the way. Every planet and symbol and their connections to one another can be considered as part of a "contract" that your soul entered into between lifetimes. The idea is that you were born when the planets aligned to create just the right energetic palette, represented in the birth chart, that would help you deliver on your commitment. In fact, one can look at every single one of those symbols as reflecting a dimension of the wounding, something we came into this lifetime to work on. As Steven Forrest says, "Wherever you've got planets, you've got wounds and an evolutionary method to solve them."

However, two celestial bodies – Pluto and Chiron – are the solar system standouts when it comes to representing the *karmic* carry-over wounds. For this reason, they are the "stars" of this book.

WHY PLUTO AND CHIRON?

Although they each have distinctive qualities and operate in different ways, Pluto and Chiron share characteristics that set them apart from the other planets in the birth chart.

- When healing opportunities or crises occur, Pluto and Chiron are the two celestial bodies in our solar system that are most likely to be active, having been stimulated in their natal positions in the birth chart by some planetary passage.

- They each have highly elliptical orbits that take them through and beyond other planets' orbits, something no other known planets do:

  o Pluto's official orbit lies far beyond Neptune's, yet from

time to time Pluto travels closer to the Sun than Neptune does. Beyond Neptune lies the vast field of Universal, spiritual energy where things can happen that
are outside the realm of what human consciousness and
action can grasp or create. By crossing back and forth
over Neptune's portal (orbit), Pluto brings healing, spiritual energies from "out there" in towards our earthly
world of the here and now.

o   Chiron, too small to be a planet, too large and out of
     range of the asteroid belt to be an asteroid (some call
     it a *planetoid*), orbits between Saturn, the outermost
     planet visible to the naked eye, and Uranus, the futur-
     istic planet of freedom and authenticity that is per-
     ceivable only with the use of a telescope. However, at
     times Chiron gets closer to the Sun than Saturn, and at
     other times goes out beyond Uranus' orbit, moving in
     the space between Uranus and Neptune, bridging the
     material, visible world and the entire invisible energetic
     realm of possibility.

•   Planets generally spend consistent-for-them amounts of
     time in each sign of the zodiac. For example, Jupiter spends
     an average of one year. However, the time that Pluto and
     Chiron spend in each sign varies widely. Pluto, for instance,
     spends about eleven years in the sign of Libra, but nine-
     teen and a half years in Leo. Similarly, Chiron will spend
     approximately seven years in Aries, but only two in Virgo.

•   The two are linked through myth. In both Greek and Roman
     mythology, Pluto and Chiron are half-brothers, both sons
     of Chronos (Saturn). Their stories take them separately to
     Hades, where in some versions of the myth they meet up
     with each other in the realm of the Underworld.

There are important differences between Pluto and Chiron in how they work and what they accomplish. We will be exploring all this in detail. For now, it's enough to focus on their unique and important commonalities and to remember that they exist in every birth chart, representing not only our woundedness, but the very energies and qualities that we can use to heal it.

HEALING: FIRST AND FOREMOST

Imagine that you're back in Junior High School, and every Saturday morning starts with your mother nagging you to "**Clean up that pigsty of a room** (or finish your chores, or practice the cello, or...) **or I'm not going to (drive you to** [*fill in the blank*], **buy you** [*fill in the blank*], **allow you to** [*you get the idea*]!!" Whether or not the threat ever actually materialized, the drum-beating of the theme probably never stopped and, in fact, got louder and more insistent until you did something about the assignment. It would then diminish to a dim-ish whisper until the *next* Saturday when the volume and tempo picked up again. And, over time, empty threatened consequences were empty no more.

Then, somewhere between Junior High and High School graduation something triggered a big change. Maybe it was a rainy Saturday with no social prospects. Maybe it was looking for an escaped pet gerbil lost in the clutter and confusion of your personal living space. Maybe you had tried out for first chair in the string department and didn't even make the short list. Something prompted you to face the consequences of your choices, including your part in creating the situation in the first place, and you set about making it right. You rolled up your sleeves and dug in. And once you got into it, it dawned on you that there was something that felt good about the whole undertaking. What's more, you were making progress way faster than you thought possible. Along the way, it's likely that some kind of help showed up in what felt "out of the blue," like a kid brother who pitched in to help by matching the socks and folding the shirts in the mile-high pile of clean laundry that had been shoved into a corner of your bed so you could have enough room to sleep. And *then* guess what? The drums stopped beating! And although you may not have wanted to admit it, you liked the way the room looked....AND that you could sleep in on Saturday mornings until it was time to meet up with your friends and head to the soccer game.

The example is simplistic, but it contains all the elements of what is perhaps THE most important and necessary step in the healing process:

YOU HAVE TO SHOW UP.

The choice to heal – to consciously and honestly confront the wound and your part in keeping it alive – is, and has to be, yours. We cannot change what we don't see or acknowledge. But, do this and you release energies and qualities that are *more* than you need to get the job done, power that you can use to move life forward into its full potential.

Later in these pages we will look at more general strategies, and then examine specific approaches geared to the planet involved as described by its placement in the birth chart. For now, it's enough to know that if you don't choose to show up, the drum keeps beating and beating, getting louder, and louder

So welcome to the club, walking wounded until we muster the readiness and courage to heal. The basics are covered. We're ready now to get up close and personal with Pluto, the Lord of the Underworld.

CHAPTER TWO

PLUTO: THE PLANET, THE MYTH, AND THE WOUND

"Though she is but little, she is fierce!"

WILLIAM SHAKESPEARE
MIDSUMMER NIGHT'S DREAM

IT'S HARD TO THINK OF PLUTO AND ITS RELENTLESS ENERGY AS A "SHE," BUT I can't think of any eight words in any language that could more accurately thumbnail The Lord of the Underworld than this quote.

PLUTO POWER

Every planet is energetically neutral. It's a pool of potential, and how we use it will determine whether that energy manifests positively or negatively. Although small in size, Pluto is the planetary embodiment of $E=MC^2$, Einstein's revolutionary atomic equation that explained how a small amount of matter can have the capacity to release incredible amounts of energy. Its namesake, Plutonium, is a radioactive element that operates in just this fashion. Pluto's energy is raw, no-holds-barred power, the primal force of death, rebirth, and transformation, and the positive use of it requires consciousness, caution, courage, and positive intent.

Pluto is intense. Its energy is concentrated into a powerball of possibility, radiating passion, uncanny psychological awareness, and a natural psychic attunement to the dark, including the forbidden and taboo. Everything about Pluto is uncompromising: black or white with no middle ground. There is simply nothing trivial, or frivolous, or nuanced about it. In its role as the "Truth Teller" Pluto demands radical honesty and backs that imperative up with bottomless courage to tell it like it is. Its gift for psychological understanding makes Pluto the hands-down planetary "crap detector." It operates with tremendous focus and single-mindedness, so it's not surprising that someone with a particularly strong Pluto (or Scorpio or Eighth House, because these are the sign and house associated with Pluto and embody its qualities) energy in their birth chart can be an unsettling presence at times.

Pluto offers the opportunity to actualize the best or worst of human potential: to heal, create, and evolve, or to destroy and regress. Allied to our highest intent and used positively, Pluto can deliver personal and societal wonders. But in the hands of ignorance, or evil, or madness, or used unconsciously without caution and positive intent, it can destroy those personal and collective worlds in a heartbeat. Here is just a short list of low-end expressions of Plutonic power: Manipulation. OCD behavior. Violence. Trauma. Nastiness. Predatory behavior. Revenge. Secretiveness. Jealousy and Resentment. Think Tony Soprano and the Mob.

Using its powerful energies, Pluto is insistent until it gets our attention. It rubs our noses in our own pain, unremittingly escalating the intensity of events and situations bearing on the wound it represents until we consciously step up to confront the issue. Stepping up is the trigger that releases Pluto's powerful healing abilities, giving us almost no choice but to muster our – and its – courage and "go for the gold" of healing and empowerment.

PLUTO AS SHAMAN

Shamans are healers who are able to directly access the vast sacred field of energetic and spiritual potential that lies beyond human awareness. They are special people who have undergone rigorous

preparation and training in spiritual and holistic healing practices. Like Pluto crossing through Neptune's orbit, shamans act as
intermediaries, linking one level of reality – our material, physical
world – with another, the Universe's vast field of energetic potential. Shamans access the realm of the Lord of the Underworld to
claim its buried treasure: power and secret wisdom that can be used
in the healing process. This typically involves literal or metaphoric
(only they know) voyages that take them deep below the Earth's
surface. Shamans then bring these gifts back to the natural world
and put them to use. The shamanic journey is perilous, dark, and
arduous. It involves entering states of consciousness that transcend
the logic and limitations of the earthly world. As we will see in a
little while, *we* live out elements of this shamanic journey during
important Pluto passages when we encounter experiences known
as "Dark Nights of the Soul."

In the Major Arcana of the Tarot, the Magician stands over a
table upon which are arrayed a wand, a cup, a pentacle coin with
a five-pointed star, and a sword. These represent the four elements
of life: the fire of action (wands); the water of emotion (cups);
the earth of consolidation and security (pentacles); and the air of
thought and wisdom (swords). The Magician stands with his right
arm raised upward, channeling the energies of the unseen world
down to the items on that earthly table. Pluto in its role as the
shaman IS the Magician.

PLUTO THE MYTH

Mythology can be a valuable tool for promoting psychological
and spiritual growth and transformation. Joseph Campbell, whom
many consider to be the greatest authority that ever lived on the
subject of mythology, said that myths explain how the world works
from the *soul*'s perspective. Mythological symbols speak to us from
Spirit and open us to great mysteries, showing how Universal Consciousness operates here on the earthly plane of daily life. Myths

are populated by archetypes, characters that represent personality traits and patterns of thought and action that are universal, eternal qualities of human nature. Archetypes show up throughout human history in all kinds of times, societies, and cultures, and we meet up with them when we are ready to work with what they symbolize. As Campbell said, myths and their symbols enable us to have "one foot in earth time and one in eternal time." And they are inexhaustible. We can go back to them again and again and find a new or deeper insight into our lives. Elizabeth Lesser said it this way in her book, *Broken Open:* "Our life stories are myths in the making."

Every planet in our solar system represents an archetype that is associated with one of the immortals in the great mythological pantheon of Greek and Roman gods and goddesses. For example, the myth of Aphrodite (*Venus*)* is about the goddess of love, beauty, artistry, and fertility who was born out of the foam of the sea, captured forever by Botticelli 's masterpiece that depicts her standing naked on a scallop shell. The archetypal qualities associated with Aphrodite the goddess are core to the interpretation of Venus the planet, and also to the goddess when she shows up in the Tarot as The Empress, or as the heroine in the latest Hollywood "rom-com."

So, we come to Hades (*Pluto*), known as the "Lord of the Underworld." (That name alone sure sets a tone, doesn't it?) Like many of the Greek myths, this one is not for the faint of heart. It starts with the Battle of the Titans between the elder and younger generations of the Olympian deities. Chronos (*Saturn*) believed that his power and authority were threatened by the birth of his sons Hades (*Pluto*) and Poseidon (*Neptune*), so he swallowed them, but was later forced to regurgitate them. Hades and Poseidon then joined up with their brother Zeus (*Jupiter*) to overthrow their father and take control.

After their victory, the brothers drew lots to divide all of creation among themselves. Zeus got the sky, Poseidon the sea, and

---

* Greek names are typically used when referencing the myths. Roman equivalents, which are used to name the planets, are italicized and in parentheses in this chapter.

Hades the underworld, a powerful, rich, dark, threatening, and mysterious realm, which was named for its master. It was a place of great buried riches, but also where the dead came to be judged: rewarded for a good life by being sent to the Elysian Fields, or punished grievously and eternally for their misdeeds.

Probably the best-known story involving Hades is about how he abducted Persephone (*Proserpina*), the daughter of Zeus and the harvest goddess Demeter (*Ceres*)* to be his underworld queen. Grief-stricken and furious, Demeter took revenge: crops failed, vegetation died, and the land became barren. Hunger, death and devastation prevailed until Hermes (*Mercury*), the messenger of the gods, brokered a deal so that Persephone could return to her mother and the earth could become fruitful again. However, there was one condition: Persephone could not have eaten anything while in the Underworld.

Hades didn't want to let Persephone go, so he tricked her into eating some pomegranate seeds. A new deal had to be negotiated. Persephone would stay in the Underworld with Hades for half the year and return to earth and her mother for the other half. Come spring, Demeter awakens the sleeping earth to blossom and flourish in welcome for her daughter. In autumn, when Persephone returns to Hades, the crops have been harvested and the earth goes barren once more while Demeter mourns the loss of her daughter until spring, when the cycle begins again.

The myth of Hades/Pluto is almost as full of symbolism that correlates with the qualities of the planet as the pomegranate is full of seeds:

- The fearful intensity, power, and mystery of the god and his realm. This includes the fact that the kingdom is *below* the surface of the earth, where cauldrons of powerful volcanic energies reside that can erupt and pierce through the earth's crust, just like the buried Pluto wound eventually come to the surface one way or another.

---

* Asteroids are named for both Demeter and Persephone.

- The black-and-white nature of decisions and judgments. Pluto is not a subtle, nuanced planet.

- The fruitfulness of the pomegranate as represented by the hundreds of seeds (some say 613!) in each individual fruit, which correlates with the extent and richness of Pluto's power.

- Pluto's name in both Greek and Roman versions means "wealth" or "riches," alluding to treasure in the form of rocks (gems) and minerals (gold and silver, etc.) that lie deeply buried beneath the earth's surface. This is another allusion to the great extent of Pluto's power, and to the buried treasure to be retrieved by healing the wound that guards it.

- The fact that Pluto will do what it takes (kill his father, Saturn, for one example) in the name of its goals.

As we explore Pluto's dimensions, thinking of the myth can evoke a deep-seated "knowing" of what you need to remember about the planet without having to keep a cheat sheet. It's how archetypes work. But first, a few more symbols to explore, each of which connects the planet to its core themes of death of the toxic and outworn, healing, transformation, and rebirth.

- This is the glyph, or astrological symbol, for Scorpio, the sign associated with Pluto: ♏ It represents the tail of the scorpion whose powerful, deadly sting can be used to eliminate anything that challenges or threatens it.

- The snake or serpent, who literally sheds its skin and creates a new one in order to grow, is another symbol associated with Pluto and the sign of Scorpio, alluding to how something may have to "die" in order for healing to take place. Interestingly, two snakes are wrapped around the caduceus, the winged staff that is emblematic of medicine's healing, regenerative powers. This is not a simple coincidence. The quote "A physician without knowledge of astrology has no right to call himself a physician." is found in the writings of Hippocrates, the very author of the Hippocratic oath!

- The phoenix is another symbol associated with the Lord of the Underworld. This mythological bird gets reborn in the ashes of its own flaming destruction, yet another reference to the planet's magnificent power to heal and make whole.

OK. I think we're ready to dig deeper, now, something Pluto just loves to do.

PLUTO THE WOUND

Every wound hurts, but none as deeply or painfully as the unhealed one represented by The Lord of the Underworld in our birth charts. Where it lies is an area that feels toxic, dirty, and scary, like New York's Gowanus Canal in the days it was one of the most polluted bodies of water in the United States. If you were to dip your toe in the Canal's waters, it would have felt like your whole foot might dissolve away. When you meet up with the Plutonic wound (astrologically speaking, when it is stimulated by the passage of any of the planets) something tells you that you're going to have to go to Hell and back to heal it and make it whole. However, just like your foot wouldn't have dissolved away from a quick dip in the Gowanus, you won't be vanquished by that wound. You're going to learn that the threat is not nearly as great as the resources you will release to confront and heal it. Still, digging it out into the light of day will take what feels like everything you've got: consciousness, courage, and radical determination and grit. And time: time to muster the guts to confront the challenge; time to excavate and cleanse the terrain; time to gather what it takes to retrieve the treasure and bring it to light. Time, in other words, to navigate a "Dark Night of the Soul" experience.

According to Joseph Campbell, the "Dark Night of the Soul" is an intrinsic part of the Heroic Journey, the saga of coming of age, or the quest for wholeness. Although we are each the hero of our own unique story and the details change with every telling, the bones of the Heroic Journey are *un*changing, showing up throughout virtually all of history, in all kinds of cultures and societies. An inevitable chapter describes the time when the hero loses his bearings. During this dark, lonely, confusing, and scary time the hero comes face-to-face with his worst fears: wounds, unresolved issues, mistakes, and the parts of himself that he is not proud of and wants to forget. He – or she – must cross the threshold into a dark, threatening place that triggers a mind full of worst case scenarios and a heart full of fear. If the hero takes up the challenge he will encounter the demons that guard the treasure he seeks to claim, but discovers that he has the strength and wisdom to conquer them, emerging stronger and "wholer" for the effort. In this adventure beyond the ordinary, help often shows up in the form of a mentor or guide to help the hero navigate the terrain. If he turns away, life can go on but nightmares, including the daytime variety, return to remind him of the unhealed, unclaimed part of himself that still lies buried in that dark, scary place.

Pluto's wound presents the classic transformational question: "What needs to die so that something new and positive can be born?" The confrontation with the necessity of some kind of death in and of itself could be enough to make you want to run for cover. There's no question that this minefield needs to be navigated mindfully and delicately, so we all need to hang a "Handle with Care" sign at Pluto's spot in the birth chart. But the prize for doing the work is worth whatever it takes: the release of powerful Plutonian energies that can be used to first heal the wound, and then advance in a forward direction in all of life:

- courage to face whatever happens, whenever it happens

- deep, regenerative healing and transformative energies

- great survival and crisis-management skills

- focus and determination

- profound psychological insight into yourself and others

- the capacity for deep, transcendent, transformative bonding, sexual and otherwise.

No matter how Pluto's wound manifests, or what you need to do in order to heal it, keep this thought in the forefront: Be kind and compassionate to yourself. The work is deep and hard...and absolutely worth it.

CHAPTER THREE

CHIRON: THE PLANETOID, THE MYTH, AND THE WOUND

"(Chiron) is an alchemical key to be found within each of us. Potential uses for this key are limited only by the individual who finds it."

RICHARD NOLLE
CHIRON: THE NEW PLANET IN YOUR HOROSCOPE

TOO SMALL TO BE A PLANET AND TOO LARGE TO BE AN ASTEROID, RESEM-bling a comet but having no tail, having an eccentric orbit that it travels with erratic speed, Chiron is a zodiacal maverick and out-sider, just like its mythological half man/half beast namesake. Its discovery in 1977 was a synchronous event that happened just as the holistic principle of body/mind/spirit integration was gaining traction in the Western world. Health food stores were proliferating, interests in energetic healing, herbalism, and yoga were growing, and even traditional allopathic medicine was starting to open up to the idea of an integrative, complimentary approach to healing. All of which provides a huge clue as to the energetic make-up of Chiron, which represents the archetype of "The Wounded Healer."

THE NATURE OF THE HALF MAN/HALF BEAST

Chiron's placement by house and sign and its connections to other planets and symbols in the birth chart describe the buried energetic treasure guarded by the existence of the Chironic wound. The name itself strengthens the message, coming from the Greek *"chiro – one who has hands"* (think chiropractor, for example), hinting of the practical, down-to-earth usefulness of the energy to be mined. Its erratic orbit provides additional insight. Chiron travels in the space between earthy, structured, hard-working, hands-on Saturn, the outermost planet visible to the naked eye, and future-oriented, free-wheeling Uranus, the planet that marks the opening to the invisible energetic realm of transcendent possibility and magic. As we have seen, Chiron at times crosses orbital boundaries and travels closer to the Sun than Saturn itself. At other times, it breeches Uranus' orbit to travel between that "Great Awakener" and Neptune. In so doing, Chiron integrates the realities of Saturn's material world (doing practical, responsible things like eating well, exercising, managing your money, and "taking care of business") with the vision and "out of the blue" possibilities of the trans-Uranian one, where genius ideas, spontaneous remissions, and logic-defying interventions reside. This energetic exchange also helps balance the potential excesses of both planets: Saturn's rigidity and limiting fear of change and Uranus' penchant for eccentricity, impulsivity and extremism.

So there it is, Chiron, the half man/half horse planetary embodiment of the holistic principle: integration of body, mind, and spirit; the combination of down-to-earth, useful, practical skills, talents, and knowledge and the "magic" of infinite possibility.

It's time for a trip back to Mount Olympus.

CHIRON THE MYTH

Like Hades *(Pluto)*, Chiron was a son of Chronos *(Saturn)* and the half-brother of Zeus *(Jupiter)*. He was born out of an affair that

Chronos had with Philyra, an oceanic nymph. Chronos' wife discovered what was going on, so he turned himself into a stallion and galloped off, leaving Philyra alone to give birth to Chiron. When she saw her son with the torso, head and arms of a man and the body and legs of a horse, Philyra was appalled and disgusted by his deformities and abandoned him. Together with Chronos, she thus inflicted his first wound: parental rejection.

The story of Chiron's birth is archetypal in itself. In Joseph Campbell's description of the Heroic Journey, the protagonist is often born in adverse circumstances that motivate him – or her – to embark on the quest for wholeness. That's how it was for Chiron. Like baby Moses being found in the bulrushes and rescued by one of the pharaoh's daughters, Chiron was rescued by unasked-for, unexpected help. Apollo, the god of prophecy, music, poetry and healing, found the abandoned infant and became his foster father. Apollo mentored Chiron, passing down to his earthly adopted son his own Olympian godly gifts, skills, and talents. He taught him about hunting, and war, and the arts, and ethics and medicine, and even led him through the mysteries of astrology. Coming of age, the half human/half horse creature came to embody the best of both the raw instincts and energies of the animal world and the wisdom and consciousness of man, and he became the leader of all the centaurs.

Now, the centaurs were a rowdy bunch. I think of them as partying fraternity brothers after a big football win. Beyond their unruly merry-making and lecherous behavior, the centaurs liked a good fight and were often at war with whatever neighboring like-minded tribe they could find. Chiron, although physically their "brother," was of a different nature entirely. He was wise, righteous, and known for "just judgment" – a healer, scholar, and prophet imbued with the wisdom of body, mind, and spirit. He became not only the leader of all the centaurs, but also the gifted teacher, advisor, and mentor of Olympians such as Hercules, Achilles, and Jason the Argonaut, and the healer of injuries and illnesses for all the gods.

There are a couple of versions of how Chiron became inflicted

with the defining wound that made him the archetypal embodiment of the suffering Wounded Healer. One story presents it as
an accident caused by an incurably poisonous stray arrow shot by
Hercules during a hunt for wild boar. Another version says it was a
consciously self-inflicted wound, motivated by a deal he made with
Zeus. Either way, he took on an excruciating, unhealable wound to
a mortal part of him, his thigh, and because he was immortal thanks
to Chronos his father, the wound would be with him for eternity.

We now cut to the myth of Prometheus, the Olympian who
gave man the gift of fire, which had previously been the exclusive
privilege of the gods. Although Prometheus was mainly motivated
by trying to make humans healthier and stronger so that they could
better serve their godly masters, Zeus was outraged at this viola-
tion of his privilege and condemned Prometheus to excruciating
eternal punishment. Lashed to a rock in Hades, a vulture would
pick away at his liver all day. Overnight the organ would grow back
and heal so the vulture could repeat the evisceration the next day...
over and over again for eternity.

One version of the myth says that Chiron negotiated with
Zeus to take on his wound for eternity in exchange for letting Prometheus off the rock, which links to Chiron's self-infliction of the
poisoned arrow. Another says that he was already wounded and
agreed to descend into Hades and willingly volunteer to relinquish
his own immortality. A third says he actually took Prometheus'
spot on the rock. The common thread is that the Wounded Healer
volunteered to take on or endure a wound – or relinquish his very
life – for the sake of another. And one way or another, he sacrifices
his own abilities, potentials, and healing gifts in the process.

As with Pluto, Chiron's myth connects to its astrological significance in several ways:

- Chiron's half human/half animal nature embodies the healing
  potential of the holistic body/mind/spirit connection.

- Chiron, mentored by Apollo, acquired wisdom and practical

skills that he used to reach his full potential as a teacher, leader, and healer. He was then able to use those qualities to help others. Healing the Chironic wound enables you to do the same.

- Perhaps most importantly, the myth explains why we cannot heal unless we examine whether or not there is motivation or incentive for us to keep the Chironic wound alive. We must ask ourselves if, like Chiron, we are *volunteering* to carry it for a lifetime.

WHY PLUTO AND CHIRON? (CONTINUED)

The mythologies of Pluto and Chiron link up and reinforce their mutual prominence in any discussion of how karmic wounding is represented in the birth chart. We've already noted that they are typically active in some way when significant healing crises or opportunities occur in the biographical, experiential life; how their orbits cause both of them to cross over other planets' orbits; and how they each in their own way bridge the physical, observable world with the vast invisible world of Universal potential.

Now, consider *these* connections:

- Both are sons of Chronos: they are half-brothers and immortal, though Chiron is half-human and not an Olympic god.

- Both are associated with buried treasure that waits to be claimed in the healing process. The wealth and riches of the treasures found in Hades represent Pluto's deep, transformative healing energies. Chiron's treasure, also buried until we release it, lies in the wisdom and practical skills that he acquired under Apollo's mentorship. The glyph or symbol for Chiron – ⚷ – is the very key that can unlock this treasure.

- In some versions of the myth, they literally meet up in Hades when Chiron takes Prometheus' place on the rock.

CHIRON THE WOUND

Chiron's placement in the birth chart is where we can be attached to bleeding out energy, without knowing or being motivated to find out that it is in our power to end the loss. It is also where we often can do something for others that we seem unable to accomplish for ourselves. When this wound is triggered, we are likely to encounter experiences where the absence of a dormant, unclaimed skill or talent in our energetic make-up is negatively affecting the situation at hand.

Let's say you have Chiron in the sign of Gemini, the communicator, in the part of the chart representing self-confidence and the ability to assert oneself in pursuit of one's goals. You're at the weekly status meeting at work and a fellow manager presents an idea *you* developed as if it were his own. You seethe but sit tight. Perhaps you fear the possible consequences that might occur if you're taken to be a sore loser trying to gain status by discrediting a colleague. Perhaps you don't want to jeopardize your status as a team player. Whatever. For one reason or another, you don't speak up. Two weeks later, that person gets a plum assignment that will probably lead to a significant bonus, if not a promotion. You head home and dump your "life's not fair" bundle of pain on your partner. A week after that, you fall on the icy driveway, stirring an old back injury that keeps you out of commission for almost a month.

This little scenario (not a contrivance, incidentally, but an incident right out of my client files) contains just about every element of an encounter with an unhealed Chironic wound:

- The wound is to an important ability or skill – in this instance Gemini's ideas and communication skills – and prevents forward motion in the person's life. It suggests that in the karmic past the person spoke up about something and was unfairly punished for it – or lost status because of it – or was disregarded or contradicted. In this lifetime, when the wound gets triggered, situations are likely to occur that test a person's commitment to speaking up for themselves with integrity and clarity.

- There's something in us that undermines a resolve to heal. In this example, it manifests in the choice to sit tight because of possible consequences that may or may not occur, but provide the rationale for silence. Not only is the opportunity missed now, but the next time the wound is stimulated, the outward manifestations are likely to be intensified.

- A health consequence occurs. Because of the holistic body/mind/spirit connection, a sickness or accident can be the outcome when an opportunity to heal the Chironic wound is missed.

Let's write a different ending for our story. Instead of saying nothing and swallowing the stress and injustice, you catch up with your colleague as you're leaving the meeting and calmly, clearly, and privately remind him (or her) of the exact circumstances under which you shared your ideas. You don't insist on a public confession, but simply state that it's the first and last time there will a free pass on the issue, and that you will not be averse to taking it to a higher level if it happens again. Shortly afterwards, you get called into a meeting with your boss who tells you that what went on in the meeting did not go unnoticed. He shares that suspicions had been growing for some time about your colleague's behavior and assures you that he's going to "make it right." And he does.

This alternate outcome describes another quality associated with Chiron's wound: the innate potential for a quick solution. Encounters with the Plutonic wound typically require prolonged engagement where something has to die or be removed before healing can take place. With Chiron, motivation and ideas for action can come up suddenly "out of the blue," and can lead to seemingly spontaneous results.

However, the work is not complete until you use the newly-retrieved abilities and skills to pay it forward in the support of others' needs. Bringing forth the buried treasure guarded by Chiron's wound increases not only your ability to heal what has wounded *your* body/mind/spirit, but empowers you to help others heal as well. Becoming a coach or mentor to pass the torch of what you know or can do is ideal. Chiron embodied that role.

CHAPTER FOUR

TIME MARCHES ON

"The more we...surrender to the depths below our woundedness, the more the vastness holds us up. There is no way to know this but to dive."

MARK NEPO
THE BOOK OF AWAKENING

HOW IT ALL WORKS

At the moment of your birth, the pattern of the planets in their signs and houses, and their connections to one another are captured for a lifetime in your astrological natal chart. However, the planets are in constant motion, each according to its own unique and totally reliable schedule, so someone born as little as fifteen minutes later than you can have measurable, significant differences in their energetic make-up.

Astrologers learn about the possibilities and challenges of any designated period of time by analyzing how the planets at *that* particular time are affecting the planets and houses of an individual's *natal* chart. Contacts between transiting (i.e. travelling) and natal planets mark opportunities for integration and healing. In all cases, two energies are trying to come together and your evolutionary need and readiness for that integration and healing triggers the synchronous mechanisms of the Universe. Circumstances or events occur without logical cause and effect connection, but they can be recognized as meaningful messages if we are tuned in and on the alert for them. Events or people appear in our everyday lives that draw our attention to the wounding: a sudden, surprising sadness at the memory of a long-ago loss; an angry over-reaction to a minor helpful suggestion that feels like an indictment of our competence; a dramatic catastrophe that almost, but doesn't quite, overwhelm and immobilize us.

Let's say that in your natal chart Venus (♀), the planet representing attraction, love, and creativity, is in the partnership-oriented sign of Libra(♎), located in the part of the chart (Fifth House) describing love affairs and romance. (A pretty juicy Venus, I'd say!) Jupiter (♃), representing abundance, expansion, confidence, and good fortune, is especially powerful in that natal chart because it is in its own sign of Sagittarius (♐), which more than doubles up all those qualities. Jupiter is natally placed in the House of Partnership (Seventh), offering the possibility that you could have positive experiences in that department. (This gets better and better, doesn't it?) These natal placements stay put throughout your lifetime.

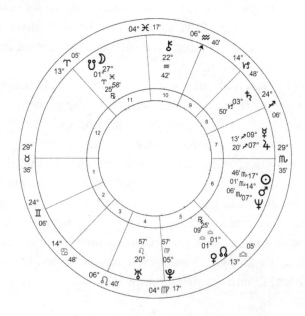

Example – Chapter 4
Natal Chart
Nov 10 1959
5:15 pm EST +5:00
New York, NY
40°N42'51" 074°W00'23"
Geocentric
Tropical
Placidus
Mean Node

Now let's imagine that you've been in something of a drought when it comes to romance for quite a while. A couple of months ago *travelling* Jupiter entered the sign of Libra, knocked at the door of that Fifth House in your chart, and stepped in to travel through it for about a year. While it is passing through the Fifth House, Jupiter is bringing the potential for abundance, expansion, and good fortune to the themes associated with that area of life, including love and romance. Maybe you start feeling like you've been too much of a shut-in and an itch to get more sociable starts to build. Then, after a while, Jupiter arrives at that Fifth House natal Venus and stays for what can be a matter of a week or a couple of months. An astrologer's jaw would not drop to the floor if your long-idle profile on a dating website started to get almost more attention than you could manage to give it. Are you going to step forward and make something happen, like setting up a few coffeehouse meet-and-greets? The energetic possibility has arrived: it's your *response* that determines the outcome and the opportunities (or lack of them) going forward.

This little episode contains all the elements of an integrative or healing opportunity:

- There is clearly-defined, unrealized potential for something (in this instance finding love in committed partnership) in the natal chart. *(Venus in Libra in the Fifth House of Romance; Jupiter in Sagittarius in the Seventh House of Partnership.)*

- The energy is dormant (you've been in a drought) until stimulated. *(Jupiter enters the Fifth House and reaches Venus.)*

- Events occur synchronously (though it might seem like it's sheer coincidence) to draw your attention to the opportunity. (The dating site profile gets activated without your intervention.)

- You must choose to show up to the opportunity. (Will you set up some introductory dates?)

This is not an all-or-nothing, one-chance-per-customer deal, because the travelling planet will return in the future, and others will pay visits. The nature of the contact describes the type and degree of effort that is required to make the most of the opportunity. Sometimes energy flows smoothly ("soft" aspects) and we can make headway without great challenge and effort, and little or no sense of urgency. Inevitably, however, there will be more stressful contacts ("hard" aspects) that create a sense of urgency, and demand grit and determination and a lot of hard work. One way or another, your *response* to the opportunity, whenever or however it presents itself, deeply affects your options the next time contact is made. If you take advantage of the smoother times, you have a leg up when the more urgent ones arrive and the Universe won't have to send you ever-escalating reminders of your unclaimed potential and/or unhealed pain.

Let's say that Mercury, the planet of thinking, learning, and communicating, is making contact with Chiron in the health and holistically-oriented sign of Virgo. A possible interpretation of that wound could include the idea that, in the karmic past, neglecting your own health incapacitated you in a way that prevented you from using innate skills as a healer. If the contact is a soft one and Mercury is flowing energy smoothly to the natal Chiron, a friend might invite you to an Introduction to Meditation workshop, and you agree to go along. There's no pressure influencing your decision, or stress and difficulty making it happen. You go, buy a couple of CDs at the program's conclusion, and start a meditation practice. At your next routine physical exam, the blood pressure numbers that had been climbing toward a medication intervention have retreated. You have learned *(Mercury)* something about how a holistic approach to health *(Chiron in Virgo)* can heal. It's been rather easy – all you had to do was say yes to an invitation. And no, the result is not a coincidence.

Now let's take the same astrological cast of characters, but change the energetic contact to a hard aspect, something that will be reflected not only in the presenting circumstances, but also in the effort required to bring about healing. You go for your annual physical fully expecting a clean bill of health, and you walk out of the doctor's office with a referral to a cardiologist. A battery of tests later, and you're told that you're a prime candidate for a double bypass, and the cardiologist is pushing hard for it. Before signing on the dotted line with a now-shaky hand, you decide to take some time to arrive at a decision. You get (conflicting) second and third opinions. You read up about the diagnosis and consult references on complementary medical approaches. You try hypnosis to lose those twenty extra pounds you've been carrying for the last ten-plus years. You bring in all kinds of information *(Mercury)* in the effort to heal a health-related wound *(Chiron in Virgo)* and, based on what you've learned, decide to go the hard route of diet, exercise, and a complementary, holistic medical approach for three months before agreeing to the more invasive one. The presenting circumstance has certainly been more urgent than a gradually-escalating increase in blood pressure, and the effort required to confront the challenge much harder.

Typically, hard and soft aspects alternate. Sometimes the healing effort will take several cycles of wound-stimulation before it is totally successful. With each contact we can make progress, dealing with the issue at a higher and higher level until the integrative, healing work is done and the released energy can be used to advance your life in other ways.

So, one last correspondence with our earlier lovelorn example:

- You *will* get another chance. (Travelling planets will enter that Fifth House and contact the Venus, but the next occasion could be announced by a more dramatic, challenging event. Heartbreak, perhaps?)

It all works the same way with Pluto and Chiron. When the wounds get stirred, it signals that you are ready: Ready to bring to consciousness something that has been blocked from awareness.

Ready to let the "monster" out of the closet so that it doesn't continue to keep you up all night and limit your life. Ready and able to do what it takes. This is especially true when either transiting Pluto or Chiron contacts its own natal position in the chart, because the healing energies of these planets are being brought to bear on the actual wounds.

So how can you recognize that the time for action has come? As is its way, our benevolent Universe is happy to deliver some clues. We have just seen one of its biggest resources in play: synchronicity. Let's suppose your wound has something to do with betrayal by a lover in the karmic past. It has left a long shadow of failed relationships in this lifetime because, for reasons having nothing to do with the actual integrity of the individual, you just can't bring yourself to trust anyone who could be a potential partner. You're two months into the latest affair, head-over-heels because you know that this could be The One, and down-at-the-heels because you can sense that ominous feeling that you're going to run for cover and torpedo the whole deal with your own insecurities and suspicions. You're at a party in Princeton, New Jersey and meet up with an old family friend. In the course of a conversation about sailing, he mentions that he was just in a regatta in the Hamptons on Long Island and met a cool guy he'd like to set you up with for a date. And guess what? Of course…it's your new guy! Do you *really* think it's just a coincidence? Saturn the karmic teacher – or some other planet of opportunity – is likely to be contacting that wound. What are you going to do about it?

A riff on the synchronicity theme is when circumstances arise that somehow reenact in this lifetime whatever it was that wounded you in the karmic past. Here's another story right out of my consulting practice.

Julie's past life history, as represented by the karmic symbols in her birth chart, was particularly traumatic and violent. This was her story: In a time of war, her parents were killed and she, only a pre-adolescent herself, was left impoverished and without support to care for her four-year-old brother. On the run from the enemy, she had to do what it took to survive, and what it took involved sexual behavior that created a shameful, painful wound, a wound that had to be deeply buried so that she could continue to function. It never could be healed in that lifetime and was casting a long shadow on this one. As is usually the case, Julie's childhood experiences reflected the karmic challenge she needed to face. She had been sexually abused by an uncle who lived with the family. Once again, a memory had to stay deeply buried so that she could survive, and it stayed that way until her brother, returning from military service overseas, needed a place to stay for a couple of months until he got settled on his own. He moved in with Julie and her family and her nightmares started almost immediately, caused only by his simple presence. Eventually, pain and exhaustion from loss of sleep drove her to therapy and past-life hypnotic regression, which took her to a lifetime where the biographical details were somewhat different from the karmic reading, but the traumatic legacy was identical.

When things like this happen, you're caught off balance for a while. But when the buried pain bubbles up it's time to "face the music" – including what your part may be in keeping the wound alive. It's not about retribution or punishment, but it's still deep, scary business and you have to be kind and compassionate to yourself. And it bears repeating that you are ready to deal with whatever you encounter. You have what it takes to do what it takes: to face truths and not be broken by them, and to stay the course. The elegant machinery of the Universe brings the stimulation when the time is right, but time's passage alone will not accomplish the healing work. Remember: it takes lots of energy to keep the pain buried. Isn't it better to use that energy to heal?

WHICH IS WHICH?

When you hurt, you hurt. At some level, it's as simple as that. You just want the pain to end. But understanding the source and nature of the wound can help you tailor the most effective approach to heal it. Here are some clues:

- <u>The window of opportunity.</u> The fact that it takes Pluto more than five times longer than Chiron to complete a circuit through all the signs and houses of the birth chart is a good place to start. The Plutonic wound is buried deeper in our unconscious because it's more intense and toxic than the Chironic one. When Pluto's wound is unhealed, it represents a huge blockage to our ability to live out this lifetime's potential. As we have seen, bringing it to light typically involves a "Dark Night of the Soul" experience, the prolonged cathartic process where something toxic, or obsolete, or inhibiting must break down or die before healing can occur. But every time we step up and work through it, healing and empowerment are the rewards. We emerge stronger and more prepared for the next time we face the challenge (astrologically-speaking, for the next time a planet makes contact with Pluto.)

  In order to accomplish this deep work, more time and more sustained effort are required than are necessary for work on Chiron's wound. If the stimulus is coming from Pluto itself, it can take up to three years. When Chiron touches a planet in the chart, only weeks or months are involved with each episode. Rapid progress, early success and even sudden breakthroughs are possible if you step up to a Chironic opportunity to reclaim buried skills and abilities.

- <u>Motivation.</u> We go back to the myths for the next difference. Chiron willingly sacrificed his own freedom and wholeness for the sake of another, taking on a wound that he, healer of the Olympian gods, could not heal. Although we have everything we need to deal with the Chironic wound, when opportunity presents itself, the *motivation* to step up and work on it may not be there. Something elusive and indefinable can hold us back. And because the window of opportunity is relatively short during a Chronic episode, it's a lot easier to ride out any discomfort that may be present until life smooths out again than it is with a Pluto event.

With Pluto, things are always black or white. "Elusive" and "indefinable" are not in its vocabulary. The urgency and intensity of the situation demand a definitive "Yes" or "No" answer: Will you step up to the challenge or not? With Chiron, you have to be on the alert for signs that something is stirring, and consider whether you're trying to take the easy way out of the situation, which of course isn't the way out at all. Synchronous clues that Chiron is ready to release its buried gifts could be things like a sudden interest in a new, useful subject or skill, a grandchild who wants to learn to ride a horse, an invitation to a meditation class, or an opportunity to volunteer your skills to a person or situation that could use your help.

• The gold: the reward for healing. The treasure to be claimed from each wound is different. Pluto's defining characteristics are transformation and empowerment. By eliminating toxicity and blockage we claim deep, powerful, raw healing energy that we can use to move forward in life. With Chiron, the coin of the realm is in terms of skills and abilities that lie dormant in us because we are either unaware of them, or don't feel we can use them effectively or confidently. Chiron in mythology sacrificed not only his own wholeness by taking on the wound, he gave up his roles as healer and as mentor to the gods in things like philosophy, astrology, horsemanship, archery, etc. Healing Chiron's wound releases tangible, practical qualities and skills that you can use not only to move your own life forward, but in service to others who need *your* help and mentorship in order to grow themselves.

BRINGING HOME THE GOLD...
THE VITAL, PASSIONATE YOU

The treasure retrieved from the healing journey can take many specific forms: a salvaged relationship, the courage to leave an outworn, unfulfilling job, writer's block removed, vanished nightmares. The list is as long and diverse as there are wounds to be healed. But the bedrock on which all the *10,000 manifestations** rest is the impassioned life, lived by someone who feels energetic, enthusiastic, and engaged in life, no longer depleted and defeated from trying to keep the lid on their wounding and from the disruptions that are created when those wounds erupt once again.

Quoting David Brooks in his article in the October 23, 2015 edition of the *New York Times,* "Who would you be and what would you do if you weren't afraid?"

---

* A Taoist phrase referring to the many ways that the Tao appears in the physical world of the here and now.

CHAPTER 5

REBECCA'S STORY

*"Without the recognition of the soul's journey within us we
are lost and only part of what we were intended to be."*

SHIRLEY MACLAINE

In a karmic reading, a past life "story" emerges from the astrological symbolism of the individual's birth chart. These glimpses into the karmic past provide important insight into the context in which wounding occurred. I never doubt that these stories are energetically true – that they accurately reflect the inner emotional and energetic response to the literal circumstances of that past lifetime. I also never doubt that the *energetic* legacy influences the person's current lifetime in important ways. However, I do not expect those stories to be necessarily *historically* accurate. The details of the life described may never have actually happened in that relevant past lifetime.

Every now and again, though, the connections between past and present lifetimes is so exact and deeply bonded that even I, after more than thirty years of astrological counseling, am stunned. Rebecca's is one such story.

Allow me to introduce her.*

---

* For those who are interested, I've parenthetically included the astrological references that support the themes and events in Rebecca's story.

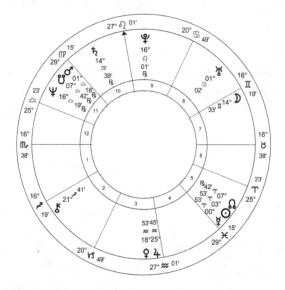

REBECCA'S STORY

When she first came to me several years ago, Rebecca was in great distress, having discovered that she had contracted a sexually transmitted disease from her philandering husband, Henry. The marriage had been an empty one for years, peppered with arguments about money, child-rearing, and Henry's narrow, oppressive definition of her role as his wife, someone whose primary job was to take care of his needs and wants in exchange for his contribution to the household expenses.

Rebecca's life had not been easy to begin with. Born into a large, traditional Catholic family, she was the only girl, and her life in the male-dominated household was about joining her very religious, compliant mother in catering to the needs and wants of her father and four brothers. She married early, thinking it was a bid for freedom, only to discover that she had jumped from frying pan into the fire.

Although she only had a high school education (the opportunity for anything more had only been available to her brothers), Rebecca was a very smart woman (*Grand Trine Air; Jupiter in Aquarius in the Third House*) and found meaningful work that she loved as a teacher's assistant in classes for students with special needs. In recent years she had gained certification in various healing modalities and had begun a long, intense course of spiritual studies in Irish shamanism (*Scorpio Rising with chart ruler Pluto in the Ninth House*). This aligned not only with her ethnic heritage but (unknown to her at the time) with the energies of her astrological birth chart. Her dream was to undertake a spiritual pilgrimage to sacred sites in Ireland (*Chart ruler Pluto in the Ninth House*), but this had to be shelved for years when her brothers *(South Node ruler Venus in the Third House)* initiated an egregiously unfounded lawsuit against her, alleging that she had robbed their widowed father while caring for him during his final illness.

After her initial consultation, Rebecca was eager to see what astrology could tell her about the relevant past lifetime, so she booked a karmic reading. Using the information from the karmic symbols in her chart, and integrating that with this lifetime's energies as represented in that chart, "Anna's" story emerged, the past-life story that was profoundly influencing Rebecca's current life. Remember, these biographical stories may never have actually happened in the historical past, but they absolutely energetically did. Before we get to it, let's learn a little about the source of the story.

THE SOUTH NODE OF THE MOON

Astrologer Steven Forrest calls the South Node of the Moon the "Eye of the Hurricane of Wounding." The placement of this astrological symbol in the birth chart provides insight into the *relevant* past lifetime, the one where the wounding occurred and whose history bears strongly on the present life. This is the symbol for the South Node: ☋. Think of it as a victory cup with handles at the top, a container that holds your karmic history and legacy. That includes the history of what went wrong or didn't get accomplished at all, along with insight into the context in which wounding occurred. A huge part of our spiritual journey in *this* lifetime is to resolve that karma and heal those wounds, so that we are no longer blocked from realizing this lifetime's potential.

The **sign** of the South Node describes attributes and qualities acquired in the karmic past and carried into this lifetime.

The **house** position of the South Node can tell us about the kinds of situations and circumstances we experienced in the karmic past, and how we acquired the qualities associated with that node.

The qualities and experiences represented by the South Node are deeply ingrained in us. Their themes resonate strongly at the unconscious, soulful level in this lifetime and, brought to consciousness, can help us understand the reasons for our wounding. What's more, we can use the knowledge, skills, and experience that we acquired in the karmic past to move forward toward this lifetime's ambitions and spiritual goals. However, precisely because of this familiarity there's a tendency to rely on South Node resources too much, and if we do that, our achievements in this lifetime could feel somehow empty. Why? Because there's no intrinsic challenge or growth potential in the South Node. We have "been there and done that."

REBECCA'S PAST LIFETIME: ANNA'S STORY

Anna had been born a fish out of water right from the start. A smart, sociable little girl, she was curious about the world around her, had blossoming creative talent, and an independent streak that was totally out of step with the rest of her family and its many children (*Grand Trine Air, including the South Node ruler, in the Third House*).

The family was part of a physically-isolated, male-dominated "tribe" out in the American West that espoused plural marriage and enforced strict rules of behavior for the women and children *(South Node in Libra in the Eleventh House; Aries Sun opposite the South Node)*. Transgressions were punished severely and arbitrarily by the male hierarchy, and Anna's mother, attuned to her child's unconventional nature and the potential difficulties it presented, worked hard to control her behavior until an early marriage could be arranged, which is what happened.

It was anything but easy for Anna to settle down and get along with her many, mostly older sister-wives *(South Node ruler Venus in the Third House)*, leaving her with even less company and support than she had had before she married. Instead of tending resolutely and obediently to her husband's demands and her household chores, or participating in wifely activities like prayer or stitching circles, she would sneak off whenever she could to the surrounding countryside with her journal and sketchbook, spending hours writing and drawing, losing track of time. Again and again the return to her husband and family brought severe restrictions that eventually escalated into harsh physical punishment *(South Node ruler Venus opposite Pluto, a karmic wound)* for her transgressions and shocking behavior *(South Node ruler in Aquarius)*. Ultimately, Anna was banished from the group, wounded not only physically *(Mars conjunct the South Node, South Node ruler opposite Pluto)*, but damaged even more profoundly in her confidence and self-esteem *(Chiron in Sagittarius in the Second House)*. This severely compromised her ability to claim the life she was born to live.

Anna's story ends there. How her life actually unfolded later is not important. The symbols suggest loss of self through escapism of some kind, or even some sort of mental imbalance *(Neptune widely conjunct the South Node)*. She probably lived in exile, traumatized and struggling unsuccessfully to fit into a culture or country dramatically different from her own *(South Node in the Eleventh House. Ruler Venus opposite Pluto in the Ninth House)*. The light of who she was or could have been was extinguished, along with her ability to take charge of her own life, and the wounds to her confidence and self-esteem *(Pluto in Leo; Chiron in the Second House)* were never healed.

• • ◆ • •

The paths of our heroines diverge as Rebecca's life unfolds in the present, but the correspondence between their stories is striking. Think of it:

- The large, male-dominated family of origin, living in accordance with religious or philosophical beliefs, rules, and restrictions

- The child that somehow didn't fit in

- The early marriage

- The heroine's disconnection and ultimate rejection by sister-wives (or brother-siblings)

- The husband as the source of profound, traumatic wounding.

REBECCA'S WOUNDS

Rebecca's birth chart has Pluto in Leo in the Ninth House. Leo is the sign associated with royalty, with people who have a strong sense of who they are and feel a fundamental rightness with having others affirm, support, and even applaud their own sense of specialness. Ruled by the Sun, Leo is confident, playful, has a great zest for life, and thrives on creative self-expression. It was precisely this sense of rightness about being and expressing who she was that was deeply wounded in Anna, and was echoed in Rebecca's early life when her own identity was so subordinated within her family. Pluto's placement in the Ninth House brings in other significant themes. This part of the birth chart represents systems that expand our understanding of how someone or something fits into a larger framework of life's meaning, systems such as philosophy, higher education, religion, and law. Ninth House themes also include long distance travel to places where we broaden our horizons by being exposed to the way people in other cultures and societies live. In the karmic past, Anna's ultimate wounding was for expressing her own individuality *(Leo)* and came in the form of being exiled by those in authority in her religion *(Pluto in Leo in the Ninth House; The Sun, ruler of Leo, opposite the South Node)*.

Rebecca's Chironic wound reinforces and expands on these themes. Her Chiron is in Sagittarius in the Second House. This sets up a linkage between the two wounds, since Sagittarius is the sign that is naturally related to the Ninth House where Pluto lies in her chart *(and Chiron trines Pluto)*. Sagittarius is associated with freedom and exploration, exactly what was so limited in both Anna's and Rebecca's lives, which were driven by familial/societal/religious rules and restrictions. The wounding attacked and eroded Anna's sense of security, and compromised her self-esteem and belief in her own value. These are Second House themes, and for Anna, the obstacles caused by this wounding were too massive to overcome. By the time her story ends she is lost, not only on alien terrain, but without a strong enough sense of herself to build a new life upon.

THIS LIFETIME: REBECCA'S STORY CONTINUES

We have seen how Rebecca was born into a contemporary version of her Libra South Node story. It is in childhood that we typically get our first introduction to the challenges, wounds, and positive legacies that are carried forward into this lifetime from our karmic past. Even Rebecca's own early marriage echoes her past life experience. The familiarity of that experience, plus the unconscious wounds that eroded confidence and self-esteem, made it unfortunately too easy for Rebecca to fall into just the patterns of behavior that would entrench her in a subservient position in relation to her husband, Henry. His oppressive, disrespectful and deceitful behavior only grew stronger with time as Rebecca gave more and more of herself away in order to meet his demands and keep the peace.

Still, Rebecca managed to carve out some space for herself, getting certified for a job she loved and pursuing her healing and spiritual studies. She was even able to put aside some money for her trip to Ireland from the modest income that came from her Reiki® practice. Something inside Rebecca knew that in *this* lifetime she could not give up her dreams because she would again lose herself in the process.

Astrologically, that something was her North Node, sitting close to the Sun in the Fifth House of her birth chart, both in the sign of Aries.

THE NORTH NODE OF THE MOON

This is the symbol for the North Node: ☊. Think of it as a set of headphones* beaming in your cosmic job description, piped in straight to you from the Universe. It is the major astrological indicator of life purpose from the spiritual perspective.

- The *sign* of the North Node describes qualities we are here to learn about, acquire, and express.

- The *house* position of the North Node describes the kinds of experiences that may occur in the course of our evolutionary growth, and in what fields of activity that growth is most

---

* Thanks to astrologer Tracy Marks for the victory cup/headphones symbolism. If you know the sign and house of your North Node, you can go to the AstrologyKarmaAndYou.com website, navigate to the "Perfect Together Additional Information" page, and learn a little about your own karmic past and the goals of your spiritual journey in this lifetime.

likely to be manifested. At least initially, we are not comfortable or sure of ourselves in this area of life experience.

The North Node draws us to it like a magnet, like our own personal True North. It's something we *feel*: a sense of purpose and intention that's not highly articulated or defined. We don't know much about where we're headed, but we know somehow that it's important to get there. We need to move toward a goal that isn't clear, leaving the safety and security of skills and qualities that we are comfortable with, and competent in, so that we can get there. What's more, the path along the way is full of experiences that challenge our basic assumptions about life, and remind us of our past life wounding.

Rebecca's North Node is in Aries. In this sign, the karmic imperative in this lifetime is to practice "Enlightened Selfishness" – to know who you are and what you need and want, and to assertively "go for it" while respecting the rights of others to do the same for themselves. Her North Node is in the Fifth House, which reinforces that theme. The Fifth House is all about celebrating who you are, bringing forth what is within you, and manifesting it in the everyday world of here and now. The overarching descriptive word associated with the Fifth House is "Creativity," and although this can certainly mean artistic accomplishment, that definition alone is far too narrow. In the broadest sense, the Fifth House is about the experiences that make you feel alive and engaged in your own life. This is why things like falling in love or giving birth to a child fall under the Fifth House umbrella.

You would expect that with this combination Rebecca's North Node would be blaring out of her chart like a Super Bowl® half-time show. Not so. Rebecca's road North was not going to be an unobstructed superhighway by a longshot. Here are some of the astrological reasons, if you're interested. If not, just skip to the next paragraph:

- Her Sun is also in the sign of Aries, and is placed close to the North Node. Although typically a Fifth House, fiery

Aries Sun is so strong it can be at risk of falling into low-end "me-first-always" aggressive and even arrogant behavior, we are born uncertain and insecure in North Node characteristics. The effect of the combination is to mute the energy of the Sun – to diminish its light – and make it hard to feel confident about Arian energy.

- Both the Sun and the Fifth House are associated with the sign of Leo and, as we have seen, Rebecca's Plutonic wound is in that sign. Every time the North Node/Sun combination is stimulated – that is, whenever Rebecca makes a move in the direction of "Enlightened Selfishness" – unconscious memories of past life wounding and trauma are stirred. Resolve and confidence in her ability to move forward are challenged.

- The Sun is opposite the South Node. The Sun is one of the symbols representing authority figures, so when the Sun and Nodes are stimulated, unconscious energetic reminders of authority figures that controlled and blocked Rebecca in her past and present lifetimes are stirred.

- Mars is the ruler, or planet, associated with the sign of Aries, the sign of her North Node. Mars sits right next to the *South* Node in Libra, giving an Arian "vibe" to the South Node. This adds a layer of mixed messages and uncertainty as to whether Rebecca is moving forward toward the North Node or back to the South Node.

KEY EVENTS

A couple of milestones in Rebecca's life reveal striking but not surprising correspondences with the karmic wounding symbols in her chart. We've already seen how her childhood was virtually a 20th Century American carbon copy of her relevant past lifetime.

(And it is not a surprise that she made the appointment for that first natal reading while the North Node/South Node axis was under pressure from Saturn, the karmic teacher.) Let's look at two defining incidents relating to the wounds.

THE LAWSUIT WAGED AGAINST
HER BY HER BROTHERS

Rebecca's Ninth House Pluto was under major stress during the two years her brothers were accusing her of robbing their dying father. (Remember, the Ninth House represents law and the justice system.) She could have easily turned away from the challenge. It was stirring not only karmic trauma and memories of what it had been like to grow up in that household in this lifetime, but she didn't even have the money to hire a lawyer. With all the complexities and pressures of her marriage tossed into the mix, the odds were definitely stacked against her. No support would be coming from that direction. But after a lot of soul-searching, Rebecca knew that she couldn't back down. She consciously made the choice to face the challenge, knowing that if circumstances went against her, at least she would know she had done all she could. She would stand up to the entire U.S. legal system if she had to, defending herself against her brothers' false accusations. So what if she only had a high school education? She knew she had an excellent brain. So what if she had no money for a lawyer? She'd take the stand herself.

The details of what Rebecca did to get ready for her day in court are staggering, and it's not important to list them all here, but at one point she asked for – and received – procedural advice from the judge himself! She went to trial lawyer-less, and gave testimony based on her legal research to be sure, but mostly she spoke straight from the heart.

The case was immediately thrown out of court, and she received her fair share of the modest inheritance. Although she barely broke even financially because of lost income and other costs associated with mounting her own defense, from the evolutionary perspective Rebecca made millions. She faced the challenge consciously and entered a Dark Night period that stirred painful memories, reminders of insecurity and confidence issues that could have stopped her dead in her tracks. She stepped into the totally alien terrain of the legal system (remember, her Pluto is in the Ninth House which represents foreign influence, "culture shock," and the law) and returned with a treasure that cannot be measured in mere dollars and cents.

THE MARRIAGE CRISIS

A few years after the lawsuit, karma once again tapped at the door of Rebecca's consciousness when she discovered during a routine gynecological exam that she had contracted a sexually transmitted disease. There was no possible source other than her husband, but that in itself was not traumatizing. It only confirmed objectively what she had known intuitively with certainty for years. And it was no surprise to discover that it was Chiron under stress this time, because of its association with health and healing.

As we have seen, Rebecca's Chiron is in freedom-loving, adventurous Sagittarius, and these qualities had been restricted in both her karmic past and the current lifetime, resulting in wounds to her self-esteem and self-confidence. This had crippled Anna's ability to create a new life for herself in the karmic past. Would Rebecca repeat the wounding in this lifetime? With Chiron, the motivation to heal is not as strong as it is with Pluto.

Rebecca had a tough decision to make. Leaving the marriage seemed to be the obvious choice, but there were children to finish raising and serious financial issues to consider. Combined, she and her husband made hardly anything more than a marginally middle-class living. It would have been easy for her to develop a rationale that allowed her to ignore the message being delivered about her Chronic wound. But she didn't. She decided to bide her time and develop a strategy to ultimately achieve the best possible outcome for herself and the kids. Before long, she did. Knowing that her husband was unlikely to have the gumption to go out on his own, she delivered an ultimatum: The marriage would be that in name only – a financial partnership and nothing more. And that meant not only changes in the bedroom. Henry would be on his own for laundry and meals, and even had to wash his own dishes in a timely manner, because Rebecca liked an orderly kitchen. He would move into the guest room immediately and be responsible for its care. If he wanted a bed instead of a pull-out couch, well, that was up to him. He would continue to contribute his established share of the household expenses. And one more thing: she would no longer be answerable to him as to how she spent her time, or about anything but her share of the common expenses when it came to money. If he decided to leave, well she couldn't control that. Her bout with her brothers had restored confidence in her ability to cope with whatever came along.

Henry initially mounted his standard counterattack, expecting that his denials, anger, and tyrannical behavior would erode her resolve and that things would go back to normal. Without a doubt, he had been totally oblivious to his wife's progress. She stood firm, issued a deadline, and outlined what she would do if he didn't comply. Henry folded his cards and agreed to the terms. Rebecca knew her man.

Just when she had finally saved enough money and booked the long-awaited trip to Ireland, Henry was involved in a fairly serious car accident on the eve of her scheduled departure. Rebecca was undeterred. After confirming that his condition was not life-threatening, she took the car service to the airport as planned. Travelling far on a spiritual pilgrimage, never having been outside the United States before, and going it alone was the perfect report card on the healing progress that she had made on *both* her karmic wounds. And she has used the energies released by her work on the Chironic wound to deepen her healing skills, paying them forward as her practice continues to grow.

EPILOGUE

The kids are almost grown now. I know that Rebecca's days in even this version of a marriage are numbered. Each time she has been presented with an opportunity to work on the wounds, each time either Pluto or Chiron has been pressured – and there have been many, great and small – she has stepped up to the challenge and emerged stronger for having taken another conscious step toward the "Enlightened Selfishness" of her Fifth House Aries North Node.

Bravo, Rebecca!

CHAPTER SIX

GOING FOR
THE GOLD

"Healing comes from…doing gladly that which I must do."

CARL JUNG

A S WE HAVE SEEN, WHEN A MOVING PLANET MAKES CONTACT WITH either Pluto or Chiron, circumstances in the outer life signal that an opportunity for healing has arrived. It's time to roll up the sleeves and hit the ground running – to go for the gold, the alchemy of transforming the dark, dense, and heavy "lead" of our wounds into the gold of what life will become as they are healed. Think of this chapter as your playbook, the tool that can help you make the most of those times.

GOING FOR THE GOLD:
GENERAL STRATEGIES

Certain basic actions and approaches apply whenever a wound is stimulated, regardless of which one it is or the nature of the contact.

- <u>Show up.</u> It all starts with this: you have a *choice* when the healing opportunity arises. You're at a crossroads and your decisions now will have far-reaching, long-lasting consequences. No one can change what they cannot or will not see. Wishing the wound away simply won't work. Neither will off-loading the pain by attributing its cause to someone or something else. It will only boomerang back and hit you even harder the next time around. Learn to recognize when you are using strategies of avoidance. What are yours? The sooner you choose to face the wound's dark music, the better.

- Be kind to yourself. Feel what you feel and then let it go. This can be a messy, painful process at times. Sometimes you'll be mourning losses or feeling guilty, or discouraged, or just plain tired. The blues can show up even after a big breakthrough, like post-partum depression after the happy event of a birth. Don't rationalize feelings away or gloss over them, but don't go to the other extreme of feeding negativity by brooding over them, either. Give yourself a real or metaphorical hug. Do something that soothes and comforts you. Forgive yourself for being human if you do come across something that needs forgiving.

- Take care of yourself. Pay attention to the needs of your body, mind, and spirit. Observe good health and diet practices. Stimulate the brain and follow where curiosity leads you to new ideas and knowledge. Connect to Spirit in ways that align with your inner leanings. It all not only strengthens you for the healing effort, but can produce long-term positive results that infuse all areas of life experience.

- Journey within. Although its symptoms manifest in the outer life, the wound and its healing energies lie within, so connection to that inner self is essential to the healing process. This requires literal peace and quiet, and practices that help clear the way to that connection, things like yoga, or meditation, or "losing" yourself in creative pursuit, or solitary walks without the earbuds. You simply can't connect to that inner voice with a ticket to NASCAR®.

- <u>Be true to yourself and the situation.</u> Don't worry about what others think. Don't compromise your integrity. Don't try to control the outcome. If you're not experiencing or getting what you want, you may be experiencing or getting exactly what you need. The Universe is holding up a mirror for you. Make this quote from sociologist and occultist Angeles Arrien your mantra for this work: "Show up. Pay attention. Tell the truth. Don't be attached to the results."

- <u>Ask for help.</u> Consult a counselor, or therapist, or trusted friend to get objective feedback. Ask the Universe for insight and support. Find someone who has mastered the skills and qualities (Chiron), or cleared themselves of wounding toxicities and blockages (Pluto), and seek their guidance. One-on-one mentorship is particularly effective with Chiron, but seeking help from those who have successfully navigated your current terrain is helpful across the board. ***You don't have to go it alone.***

- <u>Stay positive.</u> Energy that is stimulated grows stronger. Incorporate strategies that encourage optimism and confidence in your ability to get the job done. Here are a few suggestions:

  o **Affirmations.** Affirmations are present-tense, positive statements of progress and accomplishment: "I do not smoke." "The wound is healing." Craft some and say them, or better yet write them down, five times each, several times a day.

  o **Visualization.** Visualize the desired outcome: you, free of pain and what limits you, empowered with new energy and skills to make the most of your life. Personalize that vision and write a *detailed* description of it. Revisit and update it regularly.

  o **"Act as if."** Act as if what you visualize is reality. As if the healing has already been accomplished. As if you are empowered with the released energy. Start small, just outside your comfort zone, and build on the image. Don't let negativity or apathy become a self-fulfilling prophecy. Learn not to worry about things you cannot change.

- <u>Use occult and holistic tools.</u> Get read. You can put a lot together from this or any other information source about karmic wounding, but there's nothing like an astrological reading to provide fine-tuned, detailed, and personalized information about the nature of that wounding. You can learn about how it weaves into the rest of the energies in the birth chart, and acquire precise information about the timing and nature of healing opportunities and the strategies you can use to make the most of them. In Pluto times, any branch of the occult – tarot, numerology, psychic or medium readings, the *I Ching,* etc. – can provide insight and inspiration. Chiron is particularly responsive to integrative, holistic practices that unite body, mind, and spirit, such as yoga, polarity therapy, and meditation. Because Pluto and Chiron resonate with each other, you may not always know which one is crying the loudest for your attention, so it's not a bad idea to use both approaches for both wounds.

ASTROLOGY 101: THE BASICS

Before we move on to our karmic considerations, we need to take a short tour of the birth chart and its key symbols.

Your astrological birth chart, or horoscope, is the picture of the sky and its planetary inhabitants as it was at the exact moment you drew your first breath. It's as if a photographer was standing right on the delivery table with some kind of mega-magical camera pointed straight up to the sky. *"Click."* There it is: your planetary energetic picture, captured for a lifetime, in the birth chart and, more importantly, in you.

Simply stated, this birth chart is a picture of your potential for this lifetime. Its incredibly complex web of symbols represents abilities and talents and qualities related specifically to you. The chart also indicates the kinds of experiences, lessons, and opportunities to make choices that you might encounter in order to fulfill that potential. It also provides insight about roadblocks – roadblocks like karmic wounds, for example – that might slow you down or hold you back. In other words, the horoscope is one phenomenal tool that you can use to write the best story you can of this particular lifetime. To understand why you are the way you are. To take the next best step on the spiritual path.

It's your chart. No one else has it and no one else will – at least not for another 25,000 years or so. That's right, 25,000 years, and man hasn't even been on the planet that long. Unless you have an identical twin (or triplet, or, in these times, even a sextuplet) or what's called a "time twin" – someone born in the adjoining delivery room at virtually the same time as yourself – your chart is absolutely unique, and no one can actualize its potential as well as you can, because no one else lives in its energies the way you do.

The natal chart is composed of three groups of symbols:

- The Ten Planets. Each planet (the word used generically for all relevant celestial bodies: dwarf planets, planetoids, and even the Moon) represents a specific type of energy in our make-up, and every birth chart contains all ten. For example, Mars describes our individuality and sense of ourselves, our ability to assert ourselves in pursuit of our goals, and our physical energy and vitality. For our purposes, we are mainly interested in only the two symbols that represent karmic wounding:

  o **Pluto:** (♀ ♇ [Pluto can be represented by either of these symbols.]) The raw, powerful energy of transformation, empowerment, regeneration, and healing, and

- o **Chiron:** (⚷) Energy in the form of particular skills, talents, and abilities.

- The Twelve Houses. These are the pie-shaped segments in the perfectly circular 360° field of the birth chart. Houses are *where* wounding lives and healing happens. Each house represents certain areas of life experience. For example, the Seventh House is about experiences having to do with all kinds of committed partnerships, including marriage. Think in terms of *situations and circumstances* when considering house placement.

- The Twelve Signs. Signs describe *how* wounding and healing occur. They are like filters that are applied to the planets and houses, coloring and modifying the expression of their energies and experiences. Signs operate like the shade that filters the light of a lamp's bulb. Think in terms of *style* when considering how energy is expressed when filtered by its sign.

Here's an example of how the signs influence the planets. **Mercury** is the planet (energy) of thinking and communicating. Let's put it in the sign (filter) of expansive, enthusiastic **Sagittarius** and describe a sunset:

> *"Wow! What a sky-show!! The colors are unbelievable – especially the red, there, behind the clouds. Makes me wish I could be parasailing in the middle of it right now."*

Now let's take that same **Mercury**, but put it in the analytical sign of **Virgo**. Same sunset.

> *"It's 7:28 PM and the sun is less than ¼" above the horizon line. There are many cirrus clouds tonight, so the setting sun*

is starting to back-light those clouds already. The color is not quite the color of a summer tomato, but close, only with a lot more pink and gold washing through it."

One more example: the sensitive, emotional sign of **Cancer.**

"The last time I remember seeing a sunset this beautiful was on my honeymoon in Venice, 20 years ago. Those colors, reflecting on the water – like wine caught by candlelight. Thinking of that moment brings tears to my eyes."

See what I mean about the filter-factor? No one description is better than another, just different.

Using a theatrical metaphor, we can think of planets as the actors and their roles in our life story: The Hero (The Sun), The Mother (The Moon), The Teacher (Saturn), and so on. The houses can be compared to the scenery against which life's experiences play out. In the language of astrology, we might ask if it is a scene about work, or committed partnership, or security issues, themes that are all associated with particular houses in the birth chart. In the language of theatre, we'd ask if the drama took place in the office, or the bedroom, or the therapist's consulting room. Signs are like the actors' costumes, or the furniture and accessories in the stage setting. Signs give clues about the qualities associated with a particular character or scene. A woman entering from stage left in a business suit, carrying an attaché case, and calling "Mommy's home!" gives a different impression than one who's doing the dishes center-stage in her bathrobe when the curtains open.

These symbols – planets, signs, and houses – are woven into meaningful connections through their relative placement in the horoscope. They are all totally neutral, and can be expressed at any point along a continuum ranging from negative to positive. *How* they are expressed is a matter of individual free will and choice, and *not* in any way a matter of predestination.

GOING FOR THE GOLD: DRILLING DOWN

Now we can begin to focus on specifics, on details that can be learned about the nature of your own karmic wounding. Twelve tables follow that contain detailed information about Pluto and Chiron's placement by house and sign, information that describes not only the nature of the wounding, but how to recognize it and heal it. Consider the following as you review your particular tables:

- <u>First and foremost.</u> **Not every description in each category will apply to you.** That includes The Assignment. You may not have to address every aspect of it this time around. When it comes to Strategies for Healing, choose ones that align most with who you are.

- <u>Order of importance.</u> Items are listed in random order within each category, *not* in order of importance. I have tried to group related items.

- <u>Oppositions.</u> Sometimes descriptions can include distinctly opposite themes. For example, a wound to one's Leo nature can result in the person either being too egotistical and self-referential, or, alternatively, being not Leo enough: being shy and hiding their light under the bushel basket.

- <u>Theme reinforcement.</u> When your Sun (personality), Moon (emotional nature), or Rising Sign/Ascendant (style of interacting with the outside world) is in the same sign or house as either Pluto or Chiron, the effect of the wounding and sense of urgency to work on it are likely to be stronger. This also happens if either Pluto or Chiron is in a sign or house that is associated with the placement of the other wound (Examples: Pluto in the sign of Leo and Chiron in the Fifth House; Pluto and Chiron both in the sign of Virgo.) If this happens, you will have fewer tables to work with than you might have expected.

- Motivation awareness. With Chiron, you have to muster more will and determination to do the healing work. Healing is absolutely possible, but the motivation may not be there.

- Generational effect. The sign information for Pluto is generational. That is, it describes characteristics of all those born in what can be a twenty-year period. Still, the qualities of Pluto's sign and its location and interaction with the rest of the symbols in your birth chart contribute to your own *unique* energetic make-up. Knowing Pluto's house location adds a lot more personal detail, describing where the wound is stored, the areas of life experience most affected by it, and the context in which healing and empowerment can take place. It is not unusual to realize that you have been preoccupied with matters having to do with that particular house.

- Reminder. Keep in mind the general strategies described earlier in this chapter. They apply across the board:

GENERAL HEALING STRATEGIES
Show up.
Be kind to yourself.
Take care of yourself.
Journey within.
Be true to yourself and the situation.
Ask for help.
Stay positive: Affirmations. Visualization. "Act as if."
Use occult and holistic resources.

- Categories. About some of the categories in the charts:

  o **Childhood Play-Out:** Childhood circumstances and

experiences remind us of our karmic legacy, including the wounding. This section of the tables describes how you took in childhood experiences, *not necessarily how they actually were*. For example, you might have had great people as parents, people who had the best intentions and tried hard, but could not provide the unconditional love, role modeling, and guidance in ways that you could benefit from. Siblings might have had an entirely different experience with the same parents.

o **Symptoms:** These describe how you may experience the wounding and how it may affect your behavior, not only natally, but also when the wound is stimulated over time. As noted earlier, not all will apply, and some may manifest in opposite or contradictory ways.

o **The Gold You're Going For: Energies/Abilities/Skills to be Released:** It's important to keep in mind that both Pluto and Chiron hold all the energies you need (and more) to heal the wounds. That energy can then be used to advance and enhance your life in many directions and dimensions.

TO GET THE BEST RESULTS

Although you will be able to learn quite a bit directly from this book if all you know is your birth date, knowing the house placement of Pluto and Chiron will open the door to a lot more. That means using the **DATE – TIME – and PLACE** of your birth to get precisely-calculated astrological natal chart. There are many websites that will provide a free chart. **Astro.com** is one of the most accurate and reliable.

The story of a life is written in every astrological birth chart. As you review the tables that apply to you, note items that resonate, and think back to times when those themes were at play in your life. Use the information in the tables to weave a story of your healing journey. Describe how the wounding feels and how it affects your life. Include how you plan to use the strategies that "speak" to you. Imagine how life will be when wounds are healed, and how you will use the new energies that have been released. Describe it all in great detail.

If you have a copy of your chart, locate the sign and house of your North Node: ☊. Go to the **AstrologyKarmaAndYou.com** website and navigate to "Perfect Together: Additional Information." You will find a thumbnail description of your karmic history in the relevant past lifetime, and your spiritual assignment in this one. This can enrich your story with additional insight into the context in which the wounding may have occurred.

⇨ **If you know only your Date of Birth, go to "Chart 1: Pluto's Sign."** If that date falls at either end of the date range, read the adjacent sign as well to see if you resonate more to its themes or to a combination of both. (**Example:** Using the Pluto's Sign Chart, if you were born on June 10 or 11, 1958 you would read the tables for both Leo and Virgo.) Do the same with "Chart 2: Chiron's Sign."

⇨ **If you know Pluto and Chiron's sign and house positions, or have a copy of your birth chart, go directly to "Chart 3: The Tables."** Pluto is represented by one of these two symbols: ♀ ♇. This is the symbol for Chiron: ⚷

··· CHART 1: PLUTO'S SIGN ···					
BIRTH DATE	PLUTO'S SIGN		BIRTH DATE	PLUTO'S SIGN	
1900s			1900s		
05/27/14 – 10/07/37	Cancer	♋	11/06/83 – 05/18/84	Scorpio	♏
10/08/37 – 11/25/37	Leo	♌	05/19/84 – 08/27/84	Libra	♎
11/26/37 – 08/03/38	Cancer	♋	08/28/84 – 01/16/95	Scorpio	♏
08/04/38 – 02/07/39	Leo	♌	01/17/95 – 04/20/95	Sagittarius	♐
02/08/39 – 06/13/39	Cancer	♋	04/21/95 – 11/10/95	Scorpio	♏
06/14/39 – 10/20/56	Leo	♌	11/11/95 – 01/25/08	Sagittarius	♐
10/21/56 – 01/14/57	Virgo	♍	2000s		
01/15/57 – 08/18/57	Leo	♌	01/26/08 – 06/14/08	Capricorn	♑
08/19/57 – 04/11/58	Virgo	♍	06/15/08 – 11/26/08	Sagittarius	♐
04/12/58 – 06/10/58	Leo	♌	11/27/08 – 03/23/23	Capricorn	♑
06/11/58 – 10/05/71	Virgo	♍	03/24/23 – 06/11/23	Aquarius	♒
10/06/71 – 04/17/72	Libra	♎	06/12/23 – 01/20/24	Capricorn	♑
04/18/72 – 07/30/72	Virgo	♍	01/21/24 – 09/01/24	Aquarius	♒
07/31/72 – 11/05/83	Libra	♎	09/02/24 – 11/19/24	Capricorn	♑

⇨ **Continue to Chart 2**

· · · CHART 2: CHIRON'S SIGN · · ·					
BIRTH DATE	**CHIRON'S SIGN**		**BIRTH DATE**	**CHIRON'S SIGN**	
1900s			1900s		
01/29/19 – 05/24/26	Aries	♈	01/31/69 – 05/28/76	Aries	♈
05/25/26 – 10/20/26	Taurus	♉	05/29/76 – 10/13/76	Taurus	♉
10/21/26 – 03/25/27	Aries	♈	10/14/76 – 03/28/77	Aries	♈
03/26/27 – 06/06/33	Taurus	♉	03/29/77 – 06/21/83	Taurus	♉
06/07/33 – 12/22/33	Gemini	♊	06/22/83 – 11/29/83	Gemini	♊
12/23/33 – 03/23/34	Taurus	♉	11/30/83 – 04/10/84	Taurus	♉
03/24/34 – 08/27/37	Gemini	♊	04/11/84 – 06/21/88	Gemini	♊
08/28/37 – 11/22/37	Cancer	♋	06/22/88 – 07/21/91	Cancer	♋
11/23/37 – 05/28/38	Gemini	♊	07/22/91 – 09/03/93	Leo	♌
05/29/38 – 09/29/40	Cancer	♋	09/04/93 – 09/09/95	Virgo	♍
09/30/40 – 12/26/40	Leo	♌	09/10/95 – 12/29/96	Libra	♎
12/27/40 – 06/16/41	Cancer	♋	12/30/96 – 04/04/97	Scorpio	♏
06/17/41 – 07/26/43	Leo	♌	04/05/97 – 09/02/97	Libra	♎
07/27/43 – 11/17/44	Virgo	♍	09/03/97 – 01/07/99	Scorpio	♏
11/18/44 – 03/23/45	Libra	♎	01/08/99 – 06/01/99	Sagittarius	♐
03/24/45 – 07/22/45	Virgo	♍	06/02/99 – 09/21/99	Scorpio	♏
07/23/45 – 11/10/46	Libra	♎	2000s		
11/11/46 – 11/28/48	Scorpio	♏	09/22/99 – 12/11/01	Sagittarius	♐
11/29/48 – 02/08/51	Sagittarius	♐	12/12/01 – 02/21/05	Capricorn	♑
02/09/51 – 06/18/51	Capricorn	♑	02/22/05 – 07/31/05	Aquarius	♒
06/19/51 – 11/08/51	Sagittarius	♐	08/01/05 – 12/05/05	Capricorn	♑
11/09/51 – 01/27/55	Capricorn	♑	12/06/05 – 04/20/10	Aquarius	♒
01/28/55 – 03/26/60	Aquarius	♒	04/21/10 – 07/20/10	Pisces	♓
03/27/60 – 08/19/60	Pisces	♓	07/21/10 – 02/08/11	Aquarius	♒
08/20/60 – 01/20/61	Aquarius	♒	02/09/11 – 04/17/18	Pisces	♓
01/21/61 – 04/01/68	Pisces	♓	04/18/18 – 09/25/18	Aries	♈
04/02/68 – 10/18/68	Aries	♈	09/26/18 – 02/18/19	Pisces	♓
10/19/68 – 01/30/69	Pisces	♓	02/19/19 – 06/19/26	Aries	♈

⇨ **Continue to Chart 3**

Chart 3: Find the Tables that Apply to You

Every sign of the zodiac is associated with one of the twelve houses of the birth chart. Each of the following twelve tables contains information for one sign/house combination. If you only know your birth date, one or two of these tables will apply. If you know both the sign and house location for Pluto and Chiron, up to four tables could apply.

Examples:

Your chart has Pluto in Virgo in the Tenth House and Chiron in Aries in the Third House. *Four tables* would apply: the tables for Virgo, Aries, Capricorn and/or The Tenth House, and Gemini and/or The Third House.

Your chart has Pluto in Virgo in the Tenth House, and Chiron in Capricorn in the Fifth House. Only *three tables* would apply: the tables for Virgo, Capricorn and/or the Tenth House (applies twice), and Leo and/or the Fifth House. **Important:** Themes associated with the table for Capricorn and/or the Tenth House would be doubly strong.

For your convenience, signs are listed in alphabetical, not astrological, order. Jot down the page numbers for every chart that applies to you.

∙ ∙ ♦ CHART 3: THE TABLES ♦ ∙ ∙				
SIGNS			HOUSES	
SYMBOL	NAME	PAGE	#	PAGE
♒	Aquarius	Page 128	1	Page 68
♈	Aries	Page 68	2	Page 74
♋	Cancer	Page 86	3	Page 80
♑	Capricorn	Page 122	4	Page 86
♊	Gemini	Page 80	5	Page 92
♌	Leo	Page 92	6	Page 98
♎	Libra	Page 104	7	Page 104
♓	Pisces	Page 134	8	Page 110
♐	Sagittarius	Page 116	9	Page 116
♏	Scorpio	Page 110	10	Page 122
♉	Taurus	Page 74	11	Page 128
♍	Virgo	Page 98	12	Page 134

Blessings on your way,
Alice

ARIES
and/or the
FIRST HOUSE

WOUNDED IDENTITY *and* SELF-ASSERTION

PLUTO IN ARIES

CHIRON IN ARIES

Pluto has not been in the sign of Aries since 1853 and will not return to Aries until 2069

January 29, 1919 – May 24, 1926
October 21, 1926 – March 25, 1927
April 2, 1968 – October 18, 1968
January 31, 1969 – May 28, 1976
October 14, 1976 – March 28, 1977
April 18, 2018 – September 25, 2018
February 19, 2019 – June 19, 2026

REMINDERS

Signs describe the nature of the wounding and *how* healing can occur.

Houses represent the circumstances or situations affected by the wounding and *where* healing can occur.

Not every item in each category will apply to you.

If a table applies more than once, its themes should be doubled (or tripled, or even quadrupled) in strength in your considerations, according to how many times it applies to Pluto and Chiron.

AREA OF EXPERIENCE: THE FIRST HOUSE

Personality and identity. Autonomy and self-assertion. Pursuit of one's needs and goals.

Any planet in the First House of Personality gains prominence. Its energies are deeply embedded in the person's character, and they are deeply identified with those energies. When Pluto or Chiron is here, the wound is particularly powerful and can become a driving, limiting force in the personality until it is healed.

NATURE AND CAUSE OF THE WOUND

Experiences in the karmic past such as punishment and shaming for expressing or asserting yourself wounded your core identity: to feeling that it's all right to be who you are and act in pursuit of what you need or want in this lifetime.

———————•———————

THE ASSIGNMENT

To consciously and courageously embark on a mission of self-discovery. To become self-determining. To practice "enlightened selfishness:" asserting yourself towards your goals and fulfilling your legitimate needs and wants without infringing on the rights of others to do the same for themselves. To recognize and change emotional and behavioral patterns that keep wounds alive.

———————•———————

CHILDHOOD PLAY-OUT

Being criticized or punished for being yourself.

———————•———————

Being blocked or punished from pursuing your legitimate goals.

———————•———————

Lack of warmth. Conditional love. Feeling like an outsider in the family. Feelings of abandonment.

Being told to be "seen but not heard."

———————•———————

Being timid and/or a people pleaser, the "good girl or boy" who kept the peace.

———————•———————

Not going for what you want or need, or going for it and failing at it.

ARIES
and/or the
FIRST
HOUSE

Aries/First House continues...

SYMPTOMS

Compromised self-confidence and self-assurance.
These can manifest in behaviors such as:

- fear of competition, challenge or confrontation • being self-effacing
- self-doubt, sometimes masking as bravado or narcissism • exaggerated,
explosive anger, especially when frustrated or thwarted in your efforts
- championing causes on behalf of others, but not for yourself
- revolving around others' (especially partners) wishes and needs at
the expense of your own – or – the opposite behavior: relating to others as
if they don't have or aren't entitled to their own needs and wishes and/or
aggressively imposing your own on them • feeling that energy and
attention directed to yourself is selfish

**Passive-aggressive behavior.
Putting others down and
wounding *their* confidence.
Bullying or being bullied.**

Repressed emotions and
self-expression. This can become
increasingly toxic with time,
depleting energy from the effort
it takes to "keep the lid on it."

Inappropriate or unnecessary
privacy and/or secretiveness.
Moody, brooding attitude.
Having a "chip on your shoulder"
(especially when Pluto is involved.)

**Issues with anger and/or
anxiety; projecting these
qualities on others.**

ARIES
and/or the
FIRST
HOUSE

Militant self-sufficiency and/or arrogant, aggressive behavior to protect vulnerability.

Envy of others and their accomplishments; manipulation (especially when Pluto is involved.)

"Passing the buck:" shifting responsibility that should be yours to someone else.

Difficulty achieving successful outcomes as a result of behaviors such as:

- setting impossible goals • rushing in without sufficient preparation
- having a hard time making choices and acting in support of the effort
- giving up just short of victory or presuming defeat

Being accident or injury-prone.

Not liking your own body and appearance. Fatigue. Feeling awkward.

Health issues:
The sign of Aries rules the head in the physical body, so the body/mind/spirit connection can bring about symptoms like headaches, nasal congestion, or vision problems to signal the presence or stimulation of an Aries or First House wound. Fevers and rashes can also be symptomatic.

ARIES
and/or the
FIRST
HOUSE

Aries/First House continues...

STRATEGIES FOR HEALING

Find something you're passionate about and "go for it." Give yourself something you've always wanted to experience or have, as long as you don't shirk responsibility or compromise your own security, or infringe on others' rights to do that for themselves.

Face challenges and initiatives a step at a time. This lets you become acquainted with your own strengths and courage. Finish what you start.

Build relationships with people you can trust. Speak your truth and ask for objective feedback about yourself and your actions. Therapy is a particularly powerful tool for this, especially if Pluto is involved. Wounding in the First House can often draw people to you who can help you answer the questions you have about yourself.

Trust your instincts and intuition to guide you.

Cultivate self-discipline so that energy is managed once it is released.

Connect your efforts to a higher cause. Use your experience to help others discover and affirm their own sense of self and move in pursuit of their goals.

Strengthen your physical body and build vitality through strenuous, regular exercise. This also helps release repressed emotions and excess energy.

ARIES
and/or the
FIRST
HOUSE

THE GOLD YOU'RE GOING FOR: ENERGIES/ABILITIES/SKILLS TO BE RELEASED

The courage to face the challenge and the power to heal the wound.

Entrepreneurial spirit. Becoming a pioneer and trailblazer.

"Warrior energy:" the courage to "go for the gold" in your own life. A strong sense of purpose. Taking action in pursuit of your goals.

A great capacity to empower others.

The ability to balance your own needs with others'.

Good sense of timing.

Forthrightness. Decisiveness. The ability to make tough decisions in ambivalent circumstances. Strong leadership ability. Crisis management skills.

Deep psychological insight into yourself and others (especially when Pluto is involved.)

Physical energy and vitality. Good health. Resilience.

Confidence and enjoyment in your sexuality. Passion.

Feeling good about yourself. Having a strong sense of self-worth. Knowing that it's important to look out for yourself as long as it's not at the expense of others.

ARIES
and/or the
FIRST
HOUSE

[TAURUS
and/or the
SECOND HOUSE]

WOUNDED SECURITY *and* SELF-ESTEEM
WOUNDED ABILITY TO GIVE/RECEIVE LOVE
WOUNDED CREATIVITY

PLUTO IN TAURUS

Pluto has not been in
the sign of Taurus since
1854 and will not enter
that sign until 2343

CHIRON IN TAURUS

May 25, 1926 – October 20, 1926

March 26, 1927 – June 6, 1933

December 23, 1933 – March 23, 1934

May 29, 1976 – October 13, 1976

March 29, 1977 – June 21, 1983

November 30, 1983 – April 10, 1984

*Chiron does not return to
the sign of Taurus until 2027*

REMINDERS

Signs describe the nature
of the wounding and
how healing can occur.

Houses represent
the circumstances or
situations affected by
the wounding and *where*
healing can occur.

Not every item in each
category will apply to you.

If a table applies more
than once, its themes
should be doubled
(or tripled, or even
quadrupled) in strength
in your considerations,
according to how many
times it applies to Pluto
and Chiron.

AREA OF EXPERIENCE: THE SECOND HOUSE

Values and priorities (including but not
exclusively material: money, time, emotions,
energy, etc.) Material security needs.
Resource-management. Self-esteem.

NATURE AND CAUSE OF THE WOUND

Loss and deprivation in the karmic past wounded your sense of
security, safety, and self-esteem. Your ability to experience pleasure,
share affection, and appreciate and enjoy your body and its senses may also
have been affected, as well as the ability to love and/or accept love.

Taurus also represents aesthetics and creativity, so the wound may have
been incurred as a consequence of your efforts to express yourself,
leaving a legacy of blockage, lack of confidence, or self-criticism.

THE ASSIGNMENT

To build self-esteem by learning that you are autonomous and self-reliant:
that you are wise enough, creative enough, and strong enough to deal with whatever
comes along and to provide your own security, both emotionally and materially.
To examine your values and allocate your resources of every kind (material, energetic,
emotional, time, etc.) in support of those values. To open yourself up to give and
receive love, affection and passion from a position of equality with your partner.
To learn to trust your body's instinctual wisdom and have a positive relationship
with your own natural sensuality. To recognize and change emotional and
behavioral patterns that keep wounds alive.

Important: You cannot heal the relationship dimension of this wound alone.

TAURUS
and/or the
SECOND
HOUSE

Taurus/Second House continues...

CHILDHOOD PLAY-OUT

**Being made
to feel inadequate,
unimportant
or powerless.**

Extreme, unnecessary,
restrictive focus on safety
and security – or its
opposite: lack of safety
and security that
undermined those
legitimate needs in you.

Not being provided
with what you
legitimately needed
in order to thrive and
feel secure.

Being criticized
for how you look.
Body-shaming.

**Strings attached when
you were given money.**

**Being the peacemaker
at the expense of giving
yourself and your own
needs away.**

**Lack of affection
and warmth.**

SYMPTOMS

Complex situations involving money or material possessions, such as:

- power struggles or resentment over money • envy of those who have more
- being good at managing others' money or assets, but not your own
- unmanageable debt; avoidable bankruptcy; financial failure • materialism: not
knowing when "enough is enough" • equating emotional security with material
security • over-spending, especially on inessential or luxury items • making others
dependent on you for money in order to control them

**Difficulty accepting others' help.
Being concerned that there could be an ulterior motive.**

Creative blockage. Undervaluing your own creativity.

TAURUS
and/or the
SECOND
HOUSE

Love relationship issues such as:

• over-accommodation to keep the peace • feeling unlovable or unattractive
• "settling" • repeated "unlucky in love" episodes • co-dependency

Having too-literal a view of life. Not being able to see things metaphorically or symbolically.

Stubbornness, especially in defense of one's values.

Behavior and attitudes that limit your ability to promote your own healing and growth, such as:

• overvaluing others and undervaluing yourself • feeling insecure and inadequate • having an exaggerated need to prove yourself to yourself and others • being reluctant to branch forth from the status quo even when it becomes necessary or a positive opportunity presents itself

Disliking or being uncomfortable with your body and how you look.

Laziness. Procrastination.

Self-indulgent excesses: food, pleasure, luxury, etc.

Health issues:
The sign of Taurus rules the neck and throat in the physical body. The body/mind/spirit connection can bring about symptoms like a sore throat, laryngitis, or a stiff neck to signal the presence or stimulation of a Taurus or Second House wound.

TAURUS
and/or the
SECOND
HOUSE

Taurus/Second House continues...

STRATEGIES FOR HEALING

Get your finances in order. Spend wisely. Get the help you need.
(If Chiron is involved, working one-on-one with a mentor can be particularly effective.)
One's financial situation is often a barometer of self-esteem.

———————•———————

Explore these questions:

• Do you know when enough is enough? • Are you paying too much
(not necessarily money) for safety and security? Consider your relationships.
• What's important to you? What are your priorities, the order of importance
of what you value? Where are YOU on that list? (You should be at the top.)
• Does your use of all your resources (time, possessions, emotions, etc.)
line up with your values and priorities?

Cultivate prosperity-consciousness. Create a living and working environment you love and appreciate. This can be done on modest terms. Feeling good about your life circumstances increases self-esteem.

———————•———————

Expose yourself to art and beauty (especially if Taurus is involved.) Get inspired. Surrender to creative "flow:" paint a picture, write a story, decorate a room. Don't worry about an audience: this is for *you*.

Risk giving and receiving love and affection in a romantic relationship.

———————•———————

Indulge your senses responsibly: massage, aroma-therapy, soft fabrics on your skin, reasonable amounts of comfort food when you need comfort.

———————•———————

Spend time in nature. Taurus is the sign of the "Earth Spirit."

———————•———————

Learn to recognize when you're slacking off and get yourself moving.

———————•———————

Don't rush: go a step at a time. Work hard, congratulate yourself for successes, and then build on them. These wounds rock your sense of security, so don't insist on quick solutions, which can be ultimately upsetting.

TAURUS
and/or the
SECOND
HOUSE

THE GOLD YOU'RE GOING FOR: ENERGIES/ABILITIES/SKILLS TO BE RELEASED

The courage to face the challenge and the power to heal the wound.

———————•———————

Competence in the material world. Great earning power and ability to manage resources of all kinds.

———————•———————

A healthy, realistic view of what is needed to provide for your own security and safety. Knowing when "enough is enough."

———————•———————

Feeling good about yourself. Being confident. Knowing your own worth.

———————•———————

Knowing and standing up for who you are and what's important to you.

Creative ability and talent. Pleasure in creative pursuit. Aesthetic sensitivity. Good taste. (Especially when Taurus is involved.)

———————•———————

Successful personal relationships founded on mutual affection and love, regard for one another, and equality.

———————•———————

Increased flexibility and adaptability.

———————•———————

A positive attitude toward your own body and treating it accordingly. Indulging yourself appropriately and responsibly, especially from the sensory perspective: soft clothing, creams and lotions, massage, essential oils, etc.

TAURUS
and/or the
SECOND
HOUSE

GEMINI
and/or the
THIRD HOUSE

WOUNDED INTELLECT
and/or VOICE

PLUTO IN GEMINI

CHIRON IN GEMINI

Pluto has not been in the sign of Gemini since 1914 and will not return to Gemini until 2127

June 7, 1933 – December 22, 1933
March 24, 1934 – August 27, 1937
November 23, 1937 – May 28, 1938
June 22, 1983 – November 29, 1983
April 11, 1984 – June 21,1988

Chiron does not return to the sign of Gemini until 2033

REMINDERS

Signs describe the nature of the wounding and *how* healing can occur.

Houses represent the circumstances or situations affected by the wounding and *where* healing can occur.

Not every item in each category will apply to you.

If a table applies more than once, its themes should be doubled (or tripled, or even quadrupled) in strength in your considerations, according to how many times it applies to Pluto and Chiron.

AREA OF EXPERIENCE: THE THIRD HOUSE

Information-gathering.
Communication. Early Education.
Learning and teaching. Siblings.
The neighborhood and the people in it.
Short-distance travel.

NATURE AND CAUSE OF THE WOUND

Events in the karmic past wounded confidence in your intellect, in what you know, and your ability to communicate clearly, openly, and effectively. Perhaps you were punished or isolated for being a truth-teller, or criticized or shamed about your intelligence or beliefs. Your ability to trust what others tell you may also be compromised. Wounding may have involved siblings.

———●———

THE ASSIGNMENT

To follow your curiosity. To cultivate flexibility and openness to new information and ideas, and to others' points of view. To share what you know. To develop competence and confidence in your intellect and communication abilities. To resolve sibling issues. To recognize and change emotional and behavioral patterns that keep wounds alive.

———●———

CHILDHOOD PLAY-OUT

Poor communication in the family. Information and ideas that were important for you to acquire withheld or misrepresented.

———●———

Curiosity blocked or not encouraged; being punished for it.

Speech impediments: lisps, stuttering, etc.

———●———

Early education learning difficulties or insecurities.

———●———

Feeling misunderstood or criticized for your ideas.

Being lied to.

———●———

Being told to be quiet, that you were "better seen than heard."

———●———

Sibling issues: rivalry, favoritism, etc.

GEMINI
and/or the
THIRD
HOUSE

Gemini/Third House continues...

SYMPTOMS

Ineffective communication:

Not being able to express yourself clearly. Speech disorders.

Being misunderstood or encountering resistance to what you have to say.

Not realizing how you come across to others.

———————•———————

Misusing communication skills, such as:

• **withholding communication or information to retain power or manipulate (Pluto, especially)** • **using the power of words to destroy or control others' thoughts, ideas, and communication** • **using innate cleverness to mislead or deceive** • **not listening to others** • **bitter, harsh speech** • **being argumentative**

———————•———————

Extreme and/or rigid beliefs. Having a closed mind.

Needing to be "right." Rationalization.

Being pushy or defensive about your opinions.

Alternatively, the opposite may occur: insecurity about

what you know and/or reluctance to share it.

———————•———————

Intellectual insecurity (or, paradoxically intellectual arrogance, which is usually to protect vulnerability and feelings of inadequacy.)

———————•———————

Overthinking. OCD thinking and worry (especially with Pluto.)

———————•———————

GEMINI
and/or the
THIRD
HOUSE

———————•———————

Superficiality. Scattered or irrational thinking. Lack of focus or direction.
Indiscriminate acquisition of information. Inattention to detail,
or the opposite: bogged down in too much detail and information.

———————•———————

Parroting the ideas of others, believing them to be your own.

———————•———————

Nervousness. Anxiety. Restlessness.

———————•———————

Gossiping. Literally talking too much.

———————•———————

Sibling issues.

———————•———————

Travel disruptions.

———————•———————

Health issues:
The sign of Gemini rules the hands, arms, shoulders and
lungs in the physical body, so the body/mind/spirit connection
can bring about symptoms like body stiffness or aches, or problems with
manual dexterity to signal the presence or stimulation of a Gemini
or Third House wound. Thyroid issues can also be symptomatic,
as well as breathing and lung problems.

———————•———————

GEMINI
and/or the
THIRD
HOUSE

Gemini/Third House continues...

STRATEGIES FOR HEALING

"Feed the brain:" Follow your curiosity. Gather new information. Take a course or open a book on something that interests you.

Examine your ideas and beliefs. Are they really your own? Have you compromised your own point of view for the sake of acceptance? Don't shut down or become pushy when others' ideas differ from your own.

Write something: a journal, a memoire, an article about something you've learned or discovered. It could be published, but that's not the point.

Develop focus and concentration. Finish what you start.

Cultivate effective communication skills:
• Get objective feedback and professional help, if necessary. If Pluto is involved, you may not be aware of the intensity of your effect on others.
• "Tell it like it is" in a way that acknowledges the sensibilities of your audience. Don't let yourself be stifled. • Make sure that your audience understands what you are trying to communicate. • Develop good listening skills. Make sure that you understand what others are trying to communicate.

Travel beyond the immediate neighborhood. New environments and experiences expose you to new information, stimulate curiosity, and encourage a wider perspective. With this placement, you don't have to go to the ends of the earth, just beyond the familiar, everyday scene.

Teach something you know about.

Resolve sibling issues. If need be, get therapy.

NOTE: A Plutonic wound in the Third House of the birth chart is especially challenging. Although Pluto "tells it like it is," its energy is very private in terms of *what* will be communicated. This creates what can be an uncomfortable paradox because the Third House is all about openness and "spreading the word."

GEMINI
and/or the
THIRD
HOUSE

THE GOLD YOU'RE GOING FOR: ENERGIES/ABILITIES/SKILLS TO BE RELEASED

The courage to face the challenge and the power to heal the wound.

———————•———————

Open mindedness. Powerful curiosity and passion for learning. A searching mind that finds new ideas and information.

———————•———————

Quick thinking. Cleverness. Original thinking.

———————•———————

Focus. Problem-solving abilities.

———————•———————

Salesmanship. (Chiron, especially)

———————•———————

Communication power, both verbal and written. The ability to share what you know and reach diverse audiences. Good listening skills. Understanding what others are thinking and saying.

———————•———————

Talent for teaching or mentoring (Chiron, especially.)

———————•———————

Healed sibling relationships.

———————•———————

Literally, a stronger, clearer voice. Manual dexterity.

———————•———————

GEMINI
and/or the
THIRD
HOUSE

CANCER
and/or the
FOURTH HOUSE
WOUNDED EMOTIONAL SECURITY

PLUTO IN CANCER

CHIRON IN CANCER

May 27, 1914 – October 7, 1937

November 26, 1937 – August 3, 1938

February 8, 1939 – June 13, 1939

Pluto does not return to the sign of Cancer until 2057

August 28, 1937 – November 22, 1937

May 29, 1938 – September 29, 1940

December 27, 1940 – June 16, 1941

June 22, 1988 – July 21, 1991

Chiron does not return to the sign of Cancer until 2038

Note: Both Pluto and Chiron were in the sign of Cancer August 28 – October 7, 1937 and again May 29 – August 3, 1938, deeply intensifying Cancer themes for the person born during those times.

REMINDERS

Signs describe the nature of the wounding and *how* healing can occur.

Houses represent the circumstances or situations affected by the wounding and *where* healing can occur.

Not every item in each category will apply to you.

If a table applies more than once, its themes should be doubled (or tripled, or even quadrupled) in strength in your considerations, according to how many times it applies to Pluto and Chiron.

AREA OF EXPERIENCE: THE FOURTH HOUSE

Home and domestic life. The literal, physical home you live in. Early childhood. The nurturing parent (regardless of actual gender.) Ancestry and roots. Emotional security. Attunement to the inner self.

NATURE AND CAUSE OF THE WOUND

Someone or something in the karmic past rattled
(perhaps even traumatized, if Pluto is involved) your world,
resulting in self-limiting emotional issues such as insecurity,
over-sensitivity, repressed emotions, and vulnerability in
this lifetime. The ability to nurture yourself and others and/or
your confidence in that role may also have been compromised.
The family and childhood environment is a likely
setting for where this happened.

THE ASSIGNMENT

To consciously confront your emotional blockages,
vulnerabilities, and pain, and embark on the journey to heal,
giving yourself the chance to discover that you already
have everything it takes to establish and maintain your
own emotional security. To nurture and care for yourself
wisely and appropriately. To do the same for others.
To recognize and change emotional patterns
that keep wounds alive.

CANCER
and/or the
FOURTH
HOUSE

Cancer/Fourth House continues...

CHILDHOOD PLAY-OUT

NOTE: Parental roles are not gender-specific and can be split up among individuals in many ways. Other family members might well experience the same environment, including the people in it, very differently from yourself. For example, well-intentioned parents may have been able to give siblings what they needed in ways that they could accept it, but could not do the same for you.

———•———

A family environment that eroded your sense of safety and security: coldness, austerity, indifference, or abuse (especially if Pluto is involved.)

———•———

An emotionally and/or physically unavailable nurturing parent or surrogate (the person who could provide the unconditional love and acceptance that builds emotional security.) Paradoxically, this can manifest as the opposite experience: over-compensation, where parents do too much for the child, creating unhealthy dependency.

———•———

Punishment or judgmental messages when you expressed emotions.

———•———

Being cast in the role of mothering your siblings.

———•———

NOTE: When Pluto is involved, the experience can be dramatically intensified by overt power and control issues. Abuse and trauma could be involved. It bears repeating here that Pluto gives you the strength to survive whatever the circumstances were, along with the energies needed to heal and move forward in life.

———•———

SYMPTOMS

Emotional issues, such as:

• over-sensitivity, over-reaction, defensiveness • denying, hiding, or repressing your feelings • emotional distancing: retreating into a subjective "shell" that can intensify pain and worry and promote OCD-like circular thinking when sensitivities are triggered

CANCER
and/or the
FOURTH
HOUSE

• general nervousness, worry, and anxiety whose source may be hard to identify • brooding; not being able to let go of a worrisome or "negative" feeling • feeling that energy and attention directed to yourself is selfish, or the opposite: becoming a bottomless pit for emotional attention and nurturing, or tyrannizing others in the name of *your* emotional sensitivity • being so caught up in your inner world that you lose energy and become ineffective in the outer one • needing to be needed; sacrificing your own feelings, potentials, and goals; getting depleted by taking care of others' needs or demands • feeling like you've become a "ghost" in your own life • feeling – or being – rejected; experiencing emotional betrayal; finding it hard to trust others and enter relationships of your own, or going through the motions but keeping an exaggerated, self-protective emotional distance

Family issues, such as:

• **being so tied to the past and to family/ancestral values and expectations that you cannot claim your own individuality or pursue your own goals, even if you do manage to create a home and family of your own** • **repeating the wounding environment from your own childhood in the home and family you establish yourself, or never establishing one to begin with** • **difficulties in relationships with women, especially your mother or mother-surrogate** • **disconnection and alienation from your family of origin and roots** • **switching roles: mothering your parent, or letting your own child mother you**

Attracting emotionally needy people who cannot provide reciprocity or support. This can lead to "victim" mentality or becoming resentful of others' demands.

**Food issues.
Comfort food excess.**

Health issues: The sign of Cancer rules stomach, alimentary canal and breasts in the physical body, so the body/mind/spirit connection can bring on symptoms like digestive sensitivities, feeling hungry physically or metaphorically all the time, and eating disorders to signal the presence or stimulation of a Cancer or Fourth House wound.

CANCER
and/or the
FOURTH
HOUSE

Cancer/Fourth House continues...

STRATEGIES FOR HEALING

Be patient with yourself: these wounds are particularly deep and take time to heal.

"Blood to the heart, first:" Take good care of yourself. Give yourself what you need in order to feel strong, positive, safe, and secure, like plenty of rest, good food, pleasure, and relaxation.

Feel what you feel without going overboard. Sadness or pessimism are sometimes appropriate responses to what's going on. Don't judge your feelings or expect them to be logically "correct."

Claim your roots, whatever they are. Explore your ancestry. Deal with childhood issues.

Find your family and join it. The definition of *"family"* is rapidly evolving, no longer bound by classic ethnicity, gender, race, or bloodline parameters. Find "your people," so that you can participate in a mutually nurturing, caring, secure environment in which to heal and thrive.

Spend time alone. Quiet and solitude are necessary to connect to your emotions and the inner voice that can provide guidance and support. You have to *feel* your way through this work. Just don't get so caught up in that inner world that you lose touch with what's going on everywhere else.

Find someone you trust and risk emotional vulnerability. Bring issues out in the open and get objective feedback.

Therapy of all kinds, especially family therapy, is particularly helpful.

Do domestic things: cooking, home décor, de-cluttering, even cleaning. Make home a place you love to be in. Use mementoes, antiques and photographs that evoke happy memories.

Develop a positive relationship with food. Let yourself indulge reasonably (a tricky oxymoron, I know) in comfort food when you need comfort.

CANCER
and/or the
FOURTH
HOUSE

THE GOLD YOU'RE GOING FOR: ENERGIES/ABILITIES/SKILLS TO BE RELEASED

The courage to face the challenge and the power to heal the wound.

———•———

Deep psychological and emotional insight.

———•———

The ability to connect to your own feelings and accept them.

———•———

Emotional security that allows you to take care of yourself and others positively and appropriately.

———•———

Counseling and therapy skills that can be used to heal others, especially those with similar wounding. By helping others, you help yourself.

———•———

Connection with your roots and family of origin.

———•———

The ability to create and sustain secure, trustworthy, and mutually-supportive emotional relationships.

———•———

A "genius" for homemaking: great instincts about how to create the home for yourself (and those you share it with) that is a place of comfort, peace, and security.

———•———

An appropriate, healthy relationship with food.

LEO
and/or the
FIFTH HOUSE

WOUNDED CONFIDENCE *and* SELF-EXPRESSION

PLUTO IN LEO ♌ CHIRON IN LEO

October 8, 1937 – November 25, 1937

August 4, 1938 – February 7, 1939

June 14, 1939 – October 20, 1956

January 15, 1957 – August 18, 1957

April 12, 1958 – June 10, 1958

September 30, 1940 – December 26, 1940

June 17, 1941 – July 26, 1943

July 22, 1991 – September 3, 1993

Pluto does not return to the sign of Leo until 2183

Chiron does not return to the sign of Leo until 2041

REMINDERS

Signs describe the nature of the wounding and *how* healing can occur.

Houses represent the circumstances or situations affected by the wounding and *where* healing can occur.

Not every item in each category will apply to you.

If a table applies more than once, its themes should be doubled (or tripled, or even quadrupled) in strength in your considerations, according to how many times it applies to Pluto and Chiron.

Note: Both Pluto and Chiron were in the sign of Leo from September 30 through December 26, 1940 and again between June 17, 1941 and July 26, 1943 deeply intensifying Leo themes for the person born during those times.

AREA OF EXPERIENCE: THE FIFTH HOUSE

Self-expression: bringing forth what is in within you.
That which makes you feel happy to be alive. Pleasure.
Love affairs. Risk-taking. Children. Creativity.

NATURE AND CAUSE OF THE WOUND

Experiences or people in the karmic past wounded your "inner child," the spontaneous, creative, totally individual and joyful part of each of us that makes us feel alive in our own lives and seeks expression out in the world. This creates identity issues in this lifetime. Spontaneity, joy in living, confidence, creative self-expression, and the ability to love and be loved can be squelched.

THE ASSIGNMENT

To rebirth your inner child through the unselfconscious expression of your individuality. To recognize that it's OK to go for what you need in order to feel alive in your own life, as long as it doesn't infringe on the sensitivities or rights of others to do the same. To experience and share the joy of life and zest for living. To express your own uniqueness creatively in whatever way that may be. To give and receive love. To recognize and change emotional and behavioral patterns that keep wounds alive.

CHILDHOOD PLAY-OUT

Emotionally austere conditions: a joyless atmosphere; little or no affection; being ignored; spontaneity or pleasure crushed or denied.

Shaming or punishment or being ignored for expressing normal interests in sexuality.

Individuality and creativity judged, criticized, and/or suppressed. (Sometimes, the opposite is true: being uncomfortably put on display for your talents.)

Circumstances that prevented pursuit of creative interests or pleasurable experiences. (Example: financial difficulties in the family; a disabled parent or sibling.)

LEO
and/or the
FIFTH
HOUSE

Leo/Fifth House continues...

SYMPTOMS

Careless or reckless physical, emotional, or financial risk-taking (Fifth House, especially.)

———————•———————

Over-spending, especially on inessential or luxury items.

———————•———————

Self-expression in ways that are harmful or destructive to yourself or others. Dissipation. Hedonism. Irresponsible excesses in the realm of pleasure and sexuality.

Feeling special inside but not able to express that feeling positively outwardly.

———————•———————

Empty love affairs. Break-ups. Sex as performance. Expecting too much from your partners.

———————•———————

Envy of others' creative or romantic successes (Pluto, especially.)

———————•———————

Finding it hard to accept life's ordinary side. Always craving the "peak experience." Being a bottomless pit for attention. Expecting others to cater to you.

———————•———————

Suppressing self-expression or denying yourself things that give you pleasure. Not feeling confident or entitled to have the life you dream of. Hiding your light under the bushel basket. Paradoxically, the opposite scenario also applies: feelings of excess entitlement, self-dramatizing behavior, obsession with recognition and fame, self-indulgent egocentricity and pride.

LEO
and/or the
FIFTH
HOUSE

———————•———————

Blaming your parents or childhood for everything that goes wrong in your life.

———————•———————

Issues about children, such as:

• using pregnancy to control a relationship • refusing to have children because you're afraid they'll take over your life • having children and letting them take over your life • having children and not fulfilling legitimate responsibilities toward them • having children and using them as trophies or playmates

———————•———————

The "Peter Pan Syndrome:" trying to deny the natural aging process and its responsibilities instead of embracing its wisdom and opportunities.

———————•———————

Health issues: The sign of Leo rules the heart, chest, and spinal column, so the body/mind/spirit connection can bring on symptoms in these areas to signal the presence or stimulation of a Leo or Fifth House wound.

LEO
and/or the
FIFTH
HOUSE

Leo/Fifth House continues...

STRATEGIES FOR HEALING

Be yourself. Practice "enlightened selfishness:" give yourself what you need to grow and thrive as long as it doesn't impinge on the legitimate needs and wants of others.

Learn as much about yourself as you can: therapy (especially art or dance therapy,) journaling, seeking feedback from people you trust are all good places to start.

Create something just for the joy of it. It doesn't have to be artistic and it should not be for exhibition or sale, or to attract others' attention – at least at first. Lost in the process, you can get in touch with what it is that is inside of you that needs to be made visible.

Have fun. Play. Experience what gives you pleasure – as long as you don't hurt anyone else or avoid legitimate responsibilities.

"Act as if" you've completed the assignment. Energy that is stimulated grows stronger, and this strategy is particularly effective for Leo, one of the signs associated with acting. Try out for a community theatre production.

Take your inner child out to play: Spend time and have fun with young children. If circumstances are right, have a child of your own.

Fall in love, for real. Be romantic. Enjoy yourself sexually, but also consciously and responsibly.

Don't go overboard (excessive attention-mongering, childish behavior, unwise risk.)

LEO
and/or the
FIFTH
HOUSE

THE GOLD YOU'RE GOING FOR: ENERGIES/ABILITIES/SKILLS TO BE RELEASED

The courage to face the challenge and the power to heal the wound.

———————•———————

Feeling alive and confident in your own life. Expressing your authentic self. Warmth. A sunny disposition.

———————•———————

Getting in touch with your inner child:
experiencing pleasure, spontaneity, fun, and play.

———————•———————

Energy and vitality. Optimism.

———————•———————

Being comfortable and confident with creative self-expression for its own sake.
(You may find an audience, but that's not the issue.)

———————•———————

A rich, meaningful love life, both emotionally and sexually.

———————•———————

Charisma. Comfort with legitimate attention.

———————•———————

Leadership, organizational, and executive abilities.

———————•———————

Awareness of life's abundance. Generosity.

———————•———————

Love of children. Great parenting instincts and skills.

LEO
and/or the
FIFTH
HOUSE

VIRGO
and/or the
SIXTH HOUSE

WOUNDED SENSE OF COMPETENCE

PLUTO IN VIRGO

October 21, 1956 – January 14, 1957

August 19, 1957 – April 11, 1958

June 11, 1958 – October 5, 1971

April 18, 1972 – July 30, 1972

Pluto does not return to the sign of Virgo until 2202

CHIRON IN VIRGO

July 27, 1943 – November 17, 1944

March 24, 1945 – July 22, 1945

September 4, 1993 – September 9, 1995

Chiron does not return to the sign of Virgo until 2043

REMINDERS

Signs describe the nature of the wounding and *how* healing can occur.

Houses represent the circumstances or situations affected by the wounding and *where* healing can occur.

Not every item in each category will apply to you.

If a table applies more than once, its themes should be doubled (or tripled, or even quadrupled) in strength in your considerations, according to how many times it applies to Pluto and Chiron.

AREA OF EXPERIENCE: THE SIXTH HOUSE

Health, well-being, diet, and exercise.

The holistic principle and body-mind connection.

Day-to-day work: its nature and environment. Service.

Competence and skill. Hierarchal relationships (boss and employee, teacher and student, etc.) Mentoring. Pets.

NATURE AND CAUSE OF THE WOUND

Criticism of who you were and what you did in the karmic past left a wound in this lifetime of not believing you are good enough or ready enough to move forward in your own life and/or that others' needs are more important and come before your own. This can manifest as feeling in the "one down" position in all kinds of relationships, regardless of the realities of your qualities or abilities, and can lead to self-limiting, self-doubting attitudes and behaviors.

———————●———————

THE ASSIGNMENT

To persevere and develop skills and abilities that you take legitimate pride in, and can use not only to advance your own life, but also in service to others. To balance high standards with realistic expectations. To practice a holistic approach to health and healing. To benefit from mentoring and then pass the torch, mentoring others. To recognize and change emotional and behavioral patterns that keep wounds alive.

———————●———————

CHILDHOOD PLAY-OUT

Criticism. People never satisfied with what you did or how you did it.

———————●———————

No role models – or the wrong ones. No one who guided you to develop latent talents and take pride in your accomplishments.

Inappropriate responsibilities that constrained your ability to develop your own talents and/or follow your own interests.

———————●———————

Limiting illness or disability, either your own, or in the family.

Consistently having everyone else's needs taken care of before your own.

———————●———————

Being kept in an unjustified "one down" position.

VIRGO
and/or the
SIXTH
HOUSE

Virgo/Sixth House continues...

SYMPTOMS

Feeling never good enough or ready enough to risk delivering on what you're preparing to do or be. This can manifest in many ways, such as:

- over-preoccupation with details • "Analysis Paralysis" • disorganization
- perfectionism: excessively high standards • self-criticism and/or being overly-critical of others • inability to delegate • being overwhelmed by responsibilities • "spinning wheels"

———————•———————

Workaholism, drudgery, and burn-out – or the opposite: underachievement, procrastination

———————•———————

Creating so many external obligations that you can't move forward with what's important to *you*.

———————•———————

Anxiety. Nerves. Stress.

———————•———————

Feeling guilty about what you have or have not accomplished.

———————•———————

Difficulties in the workplace, especially in hierarchal relationships like boss and employee. Taking a subordinate or inferior role in work relationships, even when it isn't warranted.

———————•———————

VIRGO
and/or the
SIXTH
HOUSE

———————●———————

Serving other's needs first and never getting around to your own.
Sacrificing your own ambitions.

———————●———————

**Not taking care of yourself; embarrassment about your body
and appearance. Poor health and dietary practices.**

———————●———————

Health issues:

The sign of Virgo rules the intestines, gall bladder,

spleen, and nervous system in the physical body.

The body/mind/spirit connection can bring on symptoms

in these areas to signal the presence or stimulation of a

Virgo or Sixth House wound. Virgo and the Sixth House are

associated with the holistic principle. Auto-immune conditions

or exacerbations (Crone's disease, rheumatoid arthritis or

psoriasis, etc.) and hypochondria or psychosomatic episodes

can also present to draw attention to the wounding.

VIRGO
and/or the
SIXTH
HOUSE

Virgo/Sixth House continues...

STRATEGIES FOR HEALING

Become proficient at something you care about or that interests you. Use it for yourself, and in the service of others' needs. Balance responsibility to yourself with responsibility to others.

Find work in healing and/or service-oriented fields. Holistic initiatives that integrate the body/mind/spirit are especially favored.

Develop an appropriate relationship with work. Avoid extremes, including workaholism. Make time for R & R.

Develop a regular practice of meaningful rituals and routines. Build structure into your day.

Find someone with the skills you are trying to develop, and ask them to mentor you. Become an apprentice. Then pay it forward: become a mentor yourself.

Take good care of your body: Listen to it. Eat well. Eliminate toxicity. Get plenty of rest. Engage in holistic practices like yoga or martial arts that integrate the body/mind/spirit.

Learn to recognize and avoid excess perfectionism and ever-escalating definitions of what is acceptable. Congratulate yourself for progress and growth. Go easy on yourself.

Get a pet. Astrology has recognized the healing qualities of animals for centuries.

Rid yourself of attitudes and behaviors that stand in the way of your own growth. Identify what needs to be changed or adjusted, and what doesn't. Getting objective feedback is very helpful.

VIRGO
and/or the
SIXTH
HOUSE

THE GOLD YOU'RE GOING FOR: ENERGIES/ABILITIES/SKILLS TO BE RELEASED

The courage to face the challenge and the power to heal the wound.

———•———

Development of latent skills and talents
(especially if Chiron is involved,) such as
• the ability to "read" the body's energetic messages • holistic, integrative
healing abilities • teaching and mentoring skills • analytical strength;
common sense; strong, focused intellect • organizational skills

———•———

Having meaningful, satisfying work that transforms your own life for the better.

———•———

Being able to use your knowledge and skills to help others
advance their lives without depleting yourself.

———•———

The ability to balance responsibility to self with responsibility to others.

———•———

Knowing when to recognize a "job well done." Accepting that
some degree of imperfection is inherent in life.

———•———

Good health. Plenty of energy.

———•———

Feeling good about who you are and what you do.

LIBRA
and/or the
SEVENTH HOUSE

WOUNDED ABILITY TO HAVE SUCCESSFUL RELATIONSHIPS. WOUNDED CREATIVITY.

PLUTO IN LIBRA ♎ CHIRON IN LIBRA

PLUTO IN LIBRA

October 6, 1971 – April 17, 1972

July 31, 1972 – November 5, 1983

May 19, 1984 – August 27, 1984

Pluto does not return to the sign of Libra until 2217

CHIRON IN LIBRA

November 18, 1944 – March 23, 1945

July 23, 1945 – November 10, 1946

September 10, 1995 – December 29, 1996

April 5, 1997 – September 2, 1997

Chiron does not return to the sign of Libra until 2045

REMINDERS

Signs describe the nature of the wounding and *how* healing can occur.

Houses represent the circumstances or situations affected by the wounding and *where* healing can occur.

Not every item in each category will apply to you.

If a table applies more than once, its themes should be doubled (or tripled, or even quadrupled) in strength in your considerations, according to how many times it applies to Pluto and Chiron.

AREA OF EXPERIENCE: THE SEVENTH HOUSE

Committed relationships between equals: marriage, business partnerships, creative collaborations, best friends. What you look for in a partner. Compromise and sharing. Recognizing others' points of view.

NATURE AND CAUSE OF THE WOUND

Betrayal, manipulation, or punishment in the karmic past wounded
your ability to trust (especially if Pluto is involved) and to love and be loved for
who you are.In this lifetime, that history affects your capacity to create and sustain
healthy relationships, especially committed partnerships.

Libra also represents aesthetics and creativity, so the wound
may have been incurred as a consequence of efforts to express yourself, leaving
a legacy of blockage, lack of confidence, or self-criticism.

———•———

THE ASSIGNMENT

To become competent and confident in relationship skills: to learn to identify
trustworthy partners and risk trusting them; to share power equally; to compromise
and collaborate. To participate in relationships based on balance, commitment,
and equality, including those founded on mutual love. To learn about yourself through
relationship. To be a peace-maker without "giving yourself away." To recognize and
change emotional and behavioral patterns that keep wounds alive.

To express yourself creatively with freedom and confidence.

Important: You cannot heal the relationship dimension of this wound alone,
especially if the Seventh House is involved.

———•———

LIBRA
and/or the
SEVENTH
HOUSE

Libra/Seventh House continues...

CHILDHOOD PLAY-OUT

Parental love withdrawn if you weren't the "good girl or boy."

Abandonment by, or death of, a parent.

No role models for what constitutes a good partnership.

Trust betrayed.

Being told you were unattractive or unlovable.

Not being given appropriate, meaningful opportunities to develop social skills and ease.

Efforts at creative self-expression dismissed or criticized. Being obliged to confirm to family or societal creative standards.

SYMPTOMS

Hiding behind being nice and polite.

Over-sensitivity to others' opinions. Measuring yourself by others' standards.

Relationship issues, such as:

• staying in a relationship not good for you • choosing the wrong partner because you feel you "can't do better" • projecting your issues on the other person; not recognizing or owning your contribution to relationship challenges • having superficial or uncommitted relationships to avoid true intimacy • relationship "drama:" jealousy, power-plays, manipulation, betrayal, frequent crises (especially if Pluto is involved) • "Unlucky in Love" Syndrome: serial failed relationships

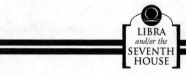

LIBRA
and/or the
SEVENTH
HOUSE

- Relationship imbalance:

choosing powerful partners who seek control, or,
the opposite – "rescuing" dependent, needy partners
that consume your energy and attention

loss of self: "giving yourself away"
to sustain the relationship, or, alternatively,
being domineering and controlling yourself

dependency issues yourself, or cultivating
dependency in your partner

———————●———————

Envy of those who
establish successful
relationships (especially
if Pluto is involved.)

———●———

Exaggerated independence
and self-sufficiency.

Lack of confidence socially.

———●———

Indecisiveness, procrastination,
endless debate without real progress.

———●———

Creative/artistic blockage
and/or self-criticism.

———————●———————

Health issues:
Libra rules the internal reproductive organs, pancreas, kidneys and
lower back in the physical body. The body/mind/spirit connection can
bring on symptoms in these areas to signal the presence or stimulation
of a Libra or Seventh House wound.

LIBRA
and/or the
SEVENTH
HOUSE

Libra/Seventh House continues...

STRATEGIES FOR HEALING

Put yourself out there. Cultivating successful relationship is not a solo assignment.
You don't have to go overboard: dip your toe in the social waters a little at a time.
Ask a relative or friend to join you if that would be helpful.

———•———

**Don't look for a partner to *complete* you. The goal is a balanced relationship
based on equality where each person *complements* the other. Make time
and space for yourself. Have things going on in your own life. Learn to know
and stand your ground. Do not give yourself away for the sake of peace.**

———•———

Take your time. Allow relationships to grow and deepen
gradually so that trust and intimacy can be established.

———•———

**Learn to recognize when you might be projecting your own issues on the
other person. Get objective feedback. Therapy is a great tool for this.**

———•———

Risk trust. If Pluto is in the Seventh House it is likely that you will have
to choose to trust someone who could potentially hurt you and share who you are
with them. Someone showing their own vulnerability is a good place to start.
Proceed slowly and build on successes: confidence grows; connections deepen.

———•———

**Examine successful relationships in your circle.
Read self-help books on the subject.**

———•———

Expose yourself to art and beauty (especially if Libra is involved.)
Get inspired. Surrender to creative "flow:" paint a picture, write a story,
decorate a room. Don't worry about an audience: This is for *you*.

LIBRA
and/or the
SEVENTH
HOUSE

THE GOLD YOU'RE GOING FOR: ENERGIES/ABILITIES/SKILLS TO BE RELEASED

The courage to face
the challenge and the power
to heal the wound.

**Being a "peace-maker"
without giving yourself away.**

**Good relationship skills
(negotiation, diplomacy,
creating and maintaining
harmony, compromise and
cooperation, balance and
equality) that can be used to
create successful relationships
of all kinds, especially
committed partnerships.**

Self-knowledge acquired through
the mirror of relationship.

**Counseling and
therapy skills.**

Social and partnership
confidence and success.

Extraordinary capacity
for deep "soul mate"
connection (especially
when Pluto is involved.)

**Artistic skills and aesthetic
sensitivities. The ability to create
beauty (especially if Libra
is involved.) Enjoyment and
fulfillment in the process.**

LIBRA
and/or the
SEVENTH
HOUSE

SCORPIO
and/or the
EIGHTH HOUSE

WOUNDED ABILITY TO CLAIM ONES POWER, TO TRUST, TO BOND DEEPLY WITH ANOTHER

PLUTO IN SCORPIO ♏ CHIRON IN SCORPIO

November 6, 1983 – May 18, 1984
August 28, 1984 – January 16, 1995
April 21, 1995 – November 10, 1995

Pluto does not return to the sign of Scorpio until 2229

November 11, 1946 – November 28, 1948
December 30, 1996 – April 4, 1997
September 3, 1997 – January 7, 1999

Chiron does not return to the sign of Scorpio until 2047

REMINDERS

Signs describe the nature of the wounding and *how* healing can occur.

Houses represent the circumstances or situations affected by the wounding and *where* healing can occur.

Not every item in each category will apply to you.

If a table applies more than once, its themes should be doubled (or tripled, or even quadrupled) in strength in your considerations, according to how many times it applies to Pluto and Chiron.

AREA OF EXPERIENCE: THE EIGHTH HOUSE

Profound transformation, empowerment, healing, and regeneration. Hidden wounds. Deep bonding and sexuality. The occult. Mystery. Research and investigation. Resources shared with others.

Scorpio and the Eighth House are naturally associated with Pluto, so the work required when these energies come together is deep and intense. When Chiron is placed in either this house or sign, the two major wounds are linked.

High stakes are involved, because these wounds are among the deepest, and major karma can be cleared.

NATURE AND CAUSE OF THE WOUND

Intense, traumatic and/or punishing experiences in the karmic past wounded your ability to claim innate healing, transformative energies. Betrayal then may make it hard to trust and enter deep, bonding relationships in this lifetime. The capacity to express yourself sexually at the deepest, most mutually empowering and transcendent levels may also be compromised.

THE ASSIGNMENT

To live the "Phoenix" experience: to consciously and courageously embark on the journey of self-discovery that leads to rebirth, transformation and empowerment. To evolve and grow through intense encounters with others that are built on radical honesty, trust, and deep bonding. To learn to share and invest all kinds of resources (money, time, energy, etc.) jointly with others. To recognize and change emotional and behavioral patterns that keep wounds alive.

CHILDHOOD PLAY-OUT

Secrets. Being lied to, manipulated, or betrayed.

Power plays. Being pressured to blindly conform to family expectations and values.

Being criticized or punished for your intense nature, or for being private with your feelings, or for your interests in sexuality or what others judged to be taboo.

Feeling you weren't wanted.

Early encounters with death.

Money issues. Material deprivation.

"Dark" premonitions. Feeling things were out of control. OCD behavior. Fear of the dark.

In the extreme: trauma, abuse, violence, abandonment.

SCORPIO and/or the EIGHTH HOUSE

Scorpio/Eighth House continues...

SYMPTOMS

Excess moodiness, defensiveness, privacy, and guardedness.

Rage: repressed or uncontrolled. Emotional isolation, usually to protect oneself.

—————•—————

Not being able to forgive. Punitive behavior. Vengeance.

—————•—————

Morbid pre-occupation with death and dying. Suicidal tendencies or thoughts.

—————•—————

Primal fears and phobias. Unhealthy preoccupation with the taboo.

Paranoia. Suspicion and superstition. Fear of the dark.

—————•—————

Relationship issues (especially in partnerships)

arising from either you or the other person, such as:

- jealousy, vindictiveness, manipulation • power struggles
- "psyching out" the other person to control the relationship, or

  the opposite: having no autonomy or control yourself
- withholding the truth, lies, betrayal of trust

—————•—————

SCORPIO
and/or the
EIGHTH
HOUSE

———•———

Issues around sexuality, such as:

• repression and insecurity, or their opposite: excess, promiscuity, compulsion • using sexuality to manipulate or control the partner • sexual bonding leading to loss of self in relationship • extreme, hazardous, or unhealthy sexual activity

———•———

Experiencing trauma or violence. Criminal activity.

———•———

Creating crises in order to manage them. Predicting or creating failure when success is on the horizon.

———•———

Money struggles, debt and/or losses, especially involving resources shared with others, such as investments, . mortgages, loans, inheritance etc.

———•———

Health issues:

Scorpio rules organs of excretion and external genitals in the physical body. Buried toxicity can be associated with the development of cancer. The body/mind/spirit connection can bring on symptoms in these areas to signal the presence or stimulation of a Scorpio or Eighth House wound.

SCORPIO
and/or the
EIGHTH
HOUSE

Scorpio/Eighth House continues...

STRATEGIES FOR HEALING

NOTE:
Deep commitment and courage are required to confront one's
wounding and embark on the shamanic healing journey with this placement.
However, because of the connection to relationship and trust issues,
this assignment cannot be completely accomplished alone.

Answer the question: "What in me must 'die' in order for me to be reborn and healed?"

Use occult resources of all kinds.

Spend time alone. This is essential in order to connect with your inner wisdom, guidance, and intuition.

Trust the gut. Develop confidence in your intuition and innate awareness or "knowing." Be open to learning from your own psychic, intuitive experiences. Expand your abilities by seeking training.

Dig deep. Profound exploration of the self and what blocks your empowerment is the prerequisite for success in this assignment. Get the support you need. Seek objective feedback about how you feel and what you intend to do. Psychotherapy is an excellent tool for this purpose.

Risk trust. Open up to intense bonding and "sacred sexuality." Find a lover who brings out and shares your passion.

Don't let others try to "lighten" you up. Your emotional intensity is an integral part of who you are. However, don't succumb to self-preoccupation and over-indulgence in your own moods.

Become responsible about money. Clear debt. Invest resources wisely and in alignment with your values, while recognizing the values of others who may be involved (partners, those to whom you are indebted, those with whom you share resources, etc.)

SCORPIO
and/or the
EIGHTH
HOUSE

THE GOLD YOU'RE GOING FOR: ENERGIES/ABILITIES/SKILLS TO BE RELEASED

The courage to face the challenge and the power to heal the wound.

————•————

Confidence. Feeling powerful, able to reach your goals and fulfill your "destiny."

————•————

The strength to look below the surface of life, confront the dark, and accept what you find.

————•————

The ability to eliminate toxicity, and to heal yourself and others. Strong regenerative energies. Long life.

————•————

Profound psychological insight into yourself and others. Counseling skills.

————•————

The ability to identify trustworthy people and to risk trusting others. To be radically trustworthy yourself.

————•————

The ability to create and maintain mutually empowering relationships.

————•————

The capacity to engage in deep, bonding sexuality.

————•————

Occult talents. Psychic awareness, and trusting its guidance.

————•————

Understanding death. Accepting its inevitability.

————•————

Crisis management skills.

————•————

Shrewd business sense and money-management skills. Actual wealth.

SCORPIO
and/or the
EIGHTH
HOUSE

SAGITTARIUS
and/or the
NINTH HOUSE

WOUNDED BELIEFS *and* FREEDOM TO EXPLORE

PLUTO IN SAGITTARIUS

CHIRON IN SAGITTARIUS

PLUTO IN SAGITTARIUS	CHIRON IN SAGITTARIUS
January 1, 1957 – April 20, 1995	November 29, 1948 – February 8, 1951
November 11, 1995 – January 25, 2008	June 19, 1951 – November 8, 1951
June 15, 2008 – November 26, 2008	January 8, 1999 – June 1, 1999
	September 22, 1999 – December 11, 2001
Pluto does not return to the sign of Sagittarius until 2241	*Chiron does not return to the sign of Sagittarius until 2049*

REMINDERS

Signs describe the nature of the wounding and *how* healing can occur.

Houses represent the circumstances or situations affected by the wounding and *where* healing can occur.

Not every item in each category will apply to you.

If a table applies more than once, its themes should be doubled (or tripled, or even quadrupled) in strength in your considerations, according to how many times it applies to Pluto and Chiron.

AREA OF EXPERIENCE: THE NINTH HOUSE

The quest for life's meaning.

Higher education and studies. Philosophy. Law. Religion.

Long distance travel and foreign influence.

Publicity and publication. Adventure.

NATURE AND CAUSE OF THE WOUND

Punishment or persecution for standing up for your beliefs in the karmic past wounded your ability in this lifetime to have confidence in your beliefs and/or intellect. Curtailment of your freedom to explore the world and find your place in it may also have occurred. Organized religion or the legal environment might have been the arena where the wounding occurred. If the wound is in the Ninth House, a foreign setting may have been involved.

THE ASSIGNMENT

To embark on a quest for meaning. To venture out into the world and expand your horizons. To discover how your life fits into a broad philosophical framework of meaning. To develop confidence and share those beliefs without being overly-assertive in trying to convert others to them. To trust your intellect and ability to organize information into meaningful patterns. To be a model for tolerance and justice. To finish what you start. To recognize and change emotional and behavioral patterns that keep wounds alive.

CHILDHOOD PLAY-OUT

Rigid, limiting religious up-bringing or its opposite: little or no religious or spiritual exposure.

Punishment for opinions or beliefs that differed from the rest of the family.

An unsettling life style with little stability or security.

Atmosphere of fear or intolerance of foreigners or anyone "different" from the family of origin.

Freedom to explore your world blocked. Punishment for your attempts to do so.

Ideas and intellect criticized or dismissed. Higher education denied.

Difficulties with long-distance or foreign travel.

SAGITTARIUS
and/or the
NINTH
HOUSE

Sagittarius/Ninth House continues...

SYMPTOMS

Issues about one's beliefs

(including, but not restricted to religious beliefs,) such as:

• cynicism; doubt; hesitancy to believe anything • rigidity; developing a philosophical justification for beliefs that may not be sound • defensiveness in support of beliefs or trying to impose them on others, or, alternatively, self-doubt. Reluctance to admit or stand for what you believe in • buying into misguided philosophical or religious causes and belief systems • espousing a religion diametrically different than the one you grew up in • limiting relationships to only those who share your own view of the world • intolerance for those who think differently from yourself

———•———

Lack of focus. Restlessness. Boredom.

Inattention to detail. Aimless wandering. Glossing over mistakes.

Not finishing what is started.

———•———

"Hoof in mouth" issues: blurting out comments or insights without consideration of the sensibilities of your audience.

———•———

SAGITTARIUS
and/or the
NINTH
HOUSE

———————•———————

Inordinate risk-taking. Pushing your luck.

———————•———————

Pushing yourself intellectually beyond limits, or the opposite: abdicating the quest for knowledge; stopping short of your educational goals or potential.

———————•———————

Legal problems, especially if they are frequent or dramatic.

———————•———————

Fear of faraway travel or foreigners. Feeling rootless, like a "stranger in a strange land."

———————•———————

Health issues:

The sign of Sagittarius rules the hips, liver, sciatic nerve
and thighs in the physical body. The body/mind/spirit connection
can bring on symptoms in these areas to signal the presence or
stimulation of a Sagittarius or Ninth House wound.

Sagittarius/Ninth House continues...

STRATEGIES FOR HEALING

Know yourself.
Examine your beliefs and attitudes…
the journey starts here.

———————•———————

Stretch the mind. Widen your world view and stretch your
boundaries with activities such as:

- pursuing higher education (not necessarily for certification or a degree;)
learning about philosophy, metaphysics, and religion, systems that provide a
framework for beliefs • adventure, exploration and travel (actual or metaphorical,)
experiencing culture shock, visiting shrines and holy, sacred places
- seeking objective, diverse feedback about your discoveries and beliefs

Risk travelling in an ever-expanding range. A step at a time is OK.	**Finish what you start in all areas.** Don't run off every time the going gets rough or boring, or a new vista grabs your attention. Pay attention to details.	Literally spend time in high places, optimally outdoors, but rooftop decks and skyscraper observation decks will do if necessary. Sagittarius, especially, flourishes from a wide-angle view in the great outdoors.
Spread the word about what you learn and discover. (Ninth House, especially.)		

SAGITTARIUS
and/or the
NINTH
HOUSE

THE GOLD YOU'RE GOING FOR: ENERGIES/ABILITIES/SKILLS TO BE RELEASED

The courage to face the challenge and the power to heal the wound.

———•———

**Freedom from limiting beliefs. Openness to others' views.
An expanded understanding of the world you live it.**

———•———

Tolerance.

———•———

Wisdom

• developing and using the "higher mind" • knowing that there's more
to life than meets the eye, that life is purposeful • "Dot Connecting:"
being able to put diverse information into meaningful patterns
• recognizing and understanding symbols and messages

———•———

Skills (Chiron, especially) in areas such as:

• disseminating information: publication, publicity, story-telling • foreign language
• law and justice • teaching (college and above, especially) • being a scholar

———•———

Openness. Being forthright and honest without being unintentionally offensive.

———•———

A sense of adventure. Exploration of life and its diversity and possibilities.

———•———

Optimism and hope for the future. Enthusiasm. Zest for living.

[CAPRICORN
and/or the
TENTH HOUSE]

WOUNDED AUTHORITY *and* ABILITY TO ACHIEVE GOALS

PLUTO IN CAPRICORN

January 26, 2008 – June 14, 2008
November 27, 2008 – March 23, 2023
June 12, 2023 – January 20, 2024

CHIRON IN CAPRICORN

February 9, 1951 – June 18, 1951
November 9, 1951 – January 27, 1955
December 12, 2001 – February 21, 2005
August 1, 2005 – December 5, 2005

Chiron does not return to the sign of Capricorn until 2052

REMINDERS

Signs describe the nature of the wounding and *how* healing can occur.

Houses represent the circumstances or situations affected by the wounding and *where* healing can occur.

Not every item in each category will apply to you.

If a table applies more than once, its themes should be doubled (or tripled, or even quadrupled) in strength in your considerations, according to how many times it applies to Pluto and Chiron.

AREA OF EXPERIENCE: THE TENTH HOUSE

Life direction, goals and career; your "mission." Public persona and reputation; your effect on those who do not know you personally. The authoritarian parent (regardless of gender.) Authority figures (boss, president, etc.)

Pluto in the Tenth House provides exceptional power with the public and the opportunity to be influential and make positive contributions to one's society and culture.

NATURE AND CAUSE
OF THE WOUND

Events and/or people in the karmic past wounded your ability
to claim authority in your own life, to achieve goals, and to make a contribution
to the world you lived in. Public reputation and respect may also have been
compromised or damaged, resulting in hesitancy to assume a public presence
or leadership role in *this* lifetime.

———————•———————

THE ASSIGNMENT

To become self-determined and claim authority and responsibility
in your own life. To gain respect. To become a leader. To achieve success in
reaching your goals. To possibly make a positive impact on the world you live in
(Tenth House, especially.) To recognize and change emotional and behavioral
patterns that keep wounds alive.

NOTE: Capricorn comes into its own with age, reaching its full potential
slowly and gradually over time. Don't be surprised or become discouraged if
there are false starts or unexpected delays along the way.

———————•———————

CAPRICORN
and/or the
TENTH
HOUSE

Capricorn/Tenth House continues...

CHILDHOOD PLAY-OUT

NOTE: Parental roles are *not* gender-specific and can be split up among individuals in many ways. Other family members might well experience the same environment, including the people in it, very differently from yourself. For example, well-intentioned parents may have been able to give siblings what they needed but could not do that for you.

———•———

No role model for achieving success, including situations such as:

• parents unsuccessful in their own lives • missing, unavailable, and/or detached authoritarian parent (this could be actual physical absence or metaphorical, as in the person being disinterested, involved in some sort of escapism, etc. • difficulties in the relationship with the authoritarian parent: conflict, defiance, misunderstandings, etc.

———•———

Unreasonable parental expectations that cannot be fulfilled.

———•———

Strict, critical, oppressive, limiting environment. Ambitions and goals not supported. Being expected to blindly conform to the "parental way" of doing things. Being bossed around.

———•———

Material and/or emotional insecurity. Austerity. Lack of warmth.

CAPRICORN
and/or the
TENTH
HOUSE

SYMPTOMS

Obsession with power and status. Autocratic behavior and/or blind ambition. Bossiness. Over-emphasis on success and recognition. A need for iron-fisted control over everyone and everything. (These may be your own behaviors, or you may encounter them in others.)

Life out of balance: all work, no play. Driving oneself. Burn-out. Over-emphasis on material and/or public success at the price of one's personal life. (Or, alternatively, holding oneself back. Being reluctant to pursue your goals or take a public role.)

Issues with the authoritarian parent (regardless of gender.) Being determined NOT to be like that person. Rage (especially when Pluto is involved) against him or her for not being what you needed.

Issues with achieving success in pursuit of your goals, such as:

• difficulty setting realistic, appropriate, achievable stretch goals • failing just short of achievement • not taking responsibility • poor decisions; "Shooting yourself in the foot." • imagining too many problems and abandoning the effort • selling oneself short • feelings of failure despite apparent success

Not having control over your own life and its direction.

Career issues: problems with superiors, being passed over for promotion, low or non-existent pay raise. Alternatively, positive developments could signal that it's time to deepen your commitment to the current path: a bonus or promotion, being assigned to a high-profile project, etc.

Health issues: The sign of Capricorn rules the skeletal structure, joints and knees in the physical body. The body/mind/spirit connection can bring on symptoms in these areas to signal the presence or stimulation of a Capricorn or Tenth House wound.

CAPRICORN and/or the TENTH HOUSE

Capricorn/Tenth House continues...

STRATEGIES FOR HEALING

Set realistic but stretch goals, not impossible standards of performance. Look for something that excites you, like making a contribution to the world you live in or achieving a long-wished for dream. Go deep: consider what could give your life purpose and meaning.

"Go for it" full-on. No one else can do this for you.

Balance personal, emotional life with ambition and career. Seek and accept responsibility and authority when the opportunity presents itself, but not at the expense of your personal life.

Be disciplined and work hard, but take care of yourself. Don't go overboard and risk burn-out.

When possible, take a leadership role. Claim your own power but cultivate sensitivity to those organizationally above and below you. Deal positively with those in authority.

Operate within "The System." Observe the existing, legitimate organizational and societal rules of the game.

Do what it takes to heal from childhood pain. Therapy is a great tool for this.

Be a truth teller.

Don't try to manipulate or control others.

Be patient. Important work takes time and time is on your side.

Seek feedback from people you trust and respect so that ambition doesn't go unrealistic or blind.

CAPRICORN
and/or the
TENTH
HOUSE

THE GOLD YOU'RE GOING FOR: ENERGIES/ABILITIES/SKILLS TO BE RELEASED

The courage to face the challenge and the power to heal the wound.

———————•———————

Commitment to achieving your life goals and ambitions. This can include a sense of "mission" especially if the Tenth House is involved.

———————•———————

Competencies you can use to work towards your goals, such as

- strategic and tactical planning skills • leadership and organizational abilities
- efficiency and productivity • "Grit:" hard work, determination and persistence; taking on responsibilities others might flee from • understanding how systems and organizations work • knowing how to operate within legitimate limits
- public speaking skills: the ability to present ideas clearly and effectively and get your message across to the audience

———————•———————

Self-respect: the satisfaction of the "job well done."

———————•———————

Taking authority in one's own life without trying to control others or encroach on their right to claim that authority for themselves.

———————•———————

The ability to foster others' growth and inspire them to achieve their own goals.

———————•———————

The energy to transform not only oneself, but others and society as well.

CAPRICORN
and/or the
TENTH
HOUSE

AQUARIUS
and/or the
ELEVENTH HOUSE
WOUNDED FREEDOM *and*
INDIVIDUALITY

PLUTO IN AQUARIUS ~~~ CHIRON IN AQUARIUS

Pluto has not been in Aquarius since 1798 and will not enter Aquarius until 2023

January 28, 1955 – March 26, 1960
August 20, 1960 – January 20, 1961
February 22, 2005 – July 31, 2005
December 6, 2005 – April 20, 2010
July 21, 2010 – February 8, 2011

Chiron does not return to the sign of Aquarius until 2055

REMINDERS

Signs describe the nature of the wounding and *how* healing can occur.

Houses represent the circumstances or situations affected by the wounding and *where* healing can occur.

Not every item in each category will apply to you.

If a table applies more than once, its themes should be doubled (or tripled, or even quadrupled) in strength in your considerations, according to how many times it applies to Pluto and Chiron.

AREA OF EXPERIENCE: THE ELEVENTH HOUSE

Participation in groups. Friends and allies: relationships based on general compatibility and mutual interests or initiatives, not close best friends. Humanitarian undertakings. Harvest themes: reaping (or not) rewards for your efforts. Hopes and wishes for the future.

NATURE AND CAUSE OF THE WOUND

Punishment and/or shaming in the karmic past for expressing
your individuality wounded your ability to express your authentic self in this lifetime.
This wounding could have come through your participation in a group activity
where you were somehow made to feel like an outsider, someone who just
didn't belong. This can leave a legacy of feeling that you never really belong
anywhere, compromising your ability to hope confidently for a life in which you
are accepted for being exactly who you are.

———————●———————

THE ASSIGNMENT

To be authentically yourself. To claim your individuality and the right
to your freedom and independence, without compromising these rights for others,
or going overboard into self-isolating extremism or eccentricity. To learn not
to be shackled by others' expectations. To take a leadership role in group initiatives
involving shared goals for social or environmental reform. To use your gift of
genius, "out-of-the-box" thinking to design the life you want to live and make a
contribution to the world you live in. To recognize and change emotional and
behavioral patterns that keep wounds alive.

NOTE: Aquarius reaches its full potential in the second half of life.
Don't be surprised or discouraged if there are false starts or unexpected
developments or delays along the way.

———————●———————

AQUARIUS
and/or the
ELEVENTH
HOUSE

Aquarius/Eleventh House continues...

129

CHILDHOOD PLAY-OUT

**Not being accepted
for who you are.**

———————•———————

Feeling like you were born into
the "wrong" family. Family member
distancing and coldness.

———————•———————

**Being excluded from
participating in group activities,
or discomfort when you did.
Not having friends.**

———————•

Feeling "weird,"
like there was something
wrong with you.

———————•———————

**Being punished,
stifled or ignored for your
original thinking.**

———————•———————

Extreme eccentric and/or
rebellious behavior.

SYMPTOMS

**Living an uncomfortable, limiting lifestyle
that is not a true reflection of who you are.**

———————•———————

Extreme eccentricity. Erratic or anti-social behavior. Rebellion.

———————•———————

Rigidity. Inflexibility. Stubbornness.

———————•———————

Denying or being disconnected from your emotions.
Needing to understand emotions logically in order to accept them
(*i.e.* living excessively out of the left side of the brain.)

AQUARIUS
and/or the
ELEVENTH
HOUSE

**Intellectual elitism: being intolerant or dismissive
of the ideas of those "not in your league."**

Not being able to identify or actualize hopes
and wishes you have for yourself.

Relationship issues, such as:

**• clashes with friends or fellow group-members • being overly-influenced by
groups, media or political or social movements • compromising who you are to
be accepted by others (or, the opposite: distancing, self-isolating behavior,
being overly-independent, having an unreasonable fear of being "overtaken" by
others, etc.) • being rejected based on who you are or what you have to say**

Not "telling it like it is." Suppressing your original ideas
to avoid criticism or rejection.

Health issues:
**The sign of Aquarius rules the calves, ankles and circulatory system
in the physical body. The body/mind/spirit connection can bring on
symptoms in these areas to signal the presence or stimulation
of an Aquarius or Eleventh House wound.**

AQUARIUS
and/or the
ELEVENTH
HOUSE

Aquarius/Eleventh House continues...

STRATEGIES FOR HEALING

Be true to yourself.

Find "your people," what Buddhists call the *sangha*. Limit or (if possible) cut relationships with those who don't accept you for who you are and who hold you back. This makes room for those who appreciate and support your individuality and freedom.

Identify what you believe in and make alliances with others who share those beliefs. Commit to a social cause.

Assume a leadership role. Don't let yourself get lost in the crowd. If you feel hesitant, "act as if" you were sure of yourself in that role and you will increasingly *become* sure of yourself. It's where you're meant to be.

Cultivate your extraordinary intelligence and originality of thought. Give yourself the freedom to explore new, radical ideas and information. Stay the course if you encounter false starts or resistance. Be true to yourself. Don't impose your beliefs on others or dismiss theirs out of hand.

Use your exceptional Aquarian brain's objectivity to give *yourself* the advice you would give your very best friend. Then follow that advice.

Let yourself feel what you feel. Don't suppress or deny emotions. Get professional help if you need it.

Cultivate flexibility. Be open to new information and others' points of view. Get feedback on your own ideas: no one knows it all.

"Go for it," whatever "it" is. Be mindful that life isn't perfect: set reasonable goals. Don't be rigidly attached to your vision of the outcome.

AQUARIUS
and/or the
ELEVENTH
HOUSE

THE GOLD YOU'RE GOING FOR: ENERGIES/ABILITIES/SKILLS TO BE RELEASED

The courage to face the challenge and the power to heal the wound.

———•———

Creative non-conformity: ability and ease expressing your individuality and "marching to your own drummer" without offending others or limiting their ability to do the same.

———•———

Exceptional group leadership and networking skills (Chiron, especially.)

———•———

"Genius" intellect. Innovative, future-oriented thinking: out-of-the-box, out-of-the-blue ideas. Objectivity and clarity.

———•———

Technological skills and innovations (Chiron, especially.)

———•———

Personal charisma. A highly-developed sense of romance.

———•———

Honesty, integrity, truth-telling. Tolerance. Being non-judgmental.

———•———

Loyalty.

———•———

A highly-developed sense of political, social and environmental potential. The skills and understanding to make a difference in the world you live in.

AQUARIUS
and/or the
ELEVENTH
HOUSE

PISCES
and/or the
TWELFTH HOUSE

WOUNDED SENSITIVITY;
LOSS OF SELF

PLUTO IN PISCES

CHIRON IN PISCES

Pluto has not been
in Pisces since 1823
and will not enter
Pisces until 2043

January 21, 1961 – April 1, 1968
October 19, 1968 – January 30, 1969
April 21, 2010 – July 20, 2010
February 9, 2011 – April 17, 2018
September 26, 2018 – February 18, 2019

REMINDERS

Signs describe the nature of the wounding and *how* healing can occur.

Houses represent the circumstances or situations affected by the wounding and *where* healing can occur.

Not every item in each category will apply to you.

If a table applies more than once, its themes should be doubled (or tripled, or even quadrupled) in strength in your considerations, according to how many times it applies to Pluto and Chiron.

AREA OF EXPERIENCE: THE TWELFTH HOUSE

Spirituality and higher levels of consciousness. The unconscious. Dreams and psychic experiences. Compassionate action. Time alone. Hospitals, jails, monasteries, etc.

Any planets in the Twelfth House are like buried treasure because they are in the unconscious at the time of birth. By definition we are unaware of them. Therefore, the challenge on the healing journey is increased when either Pluto or Chiron is in this part of the chart.

NATURE AND CAUSE OF THE WOUND

Events or people in the karmic past overwhelmed your sensitivities and wounded you deeply, causing you to shut down and "lose yourself" in any number of ways: addiction and escapism, depression, lethargy and apathy, or in the extreme, suicide. Regardless of how it happened, the result was that you did not actualize the opportunities and potential of that lifetime. Deceit may have been involved as well – on your part, or coming from others. All this may have resulted in a legacy of confusion and uncertainty in this lifetime, putting you at risk of repeating that past life scenario in some way.

———•———

THE ASSIGNMENT

To explore the unconscious, claim the strengths, and heal the wounds that may be "buried" there. To connect to Spirit and explore the world beyond the material, earthly one we live in. To learn to trust your sensitivities and intuition. To open your heart to others' suffering. To recognize and change emotional and behavioral patterns that keep wounds live.

———•———

CHILDHOOD PLAY-OUT

Family secrets. Deceit. Lack of clarity.

———•———

Addiction or escapism in the family. Failure or hard times due to apathy, procrastination, irresponsibility, etc.

———•———

Feelings of isolation. Loneliness. Confidence issues. Insecurity.

Emotional turmoil. Sensitivities not recognized and respected, or being criticized or punished for them.

———•———

Elusive, perhaps debilitating, difficult-to-diagnose illness in yourself or family members, including hypochondria and psychosomatically-based conditions.

PISCES
and/or the
TWELFTH
HOUSE

Pisces/Twelfth House continues...

SYMPTOMS

Drifting. Lack of focus. Confusion. Procrastination.
Apathy. Feeling vulnerable, powerless.

———————————●———————————

**Escapism and addiction. Sometimes this can manifest in
socially-acceptable ways, as in when workaholism results in neglect
of what one is supposed to be doing for themselves.**

———————————●———————————

Emotional overload. Feeling overwhelmed. Hypersensitivity.
Experiencing "existential grief" for pain you imagine others have. Being haunted by
past "sins" and mistakes. The opposite can also manifest: having an overly-rational,
analytical approach to emotions. Repressing or denying emotions.

———————————●———————————

Pessimism. Depression. Disillusionment.

———————————●———————————

Loss of self in relationships with others. Not following your own path,
or feeling guilty if you do. Not being able to tolerate separation from loved ones.
Envying those with a strong sense of self.

———————————●———————————

Extreme seclusion or isolation. Fear of being alone or on your own.

———————————●———————————

Negative experiences involving hospitals, shelters or jails.

PISCES
and/or the
TWELFTH
HOUSE

———•———

Sacrificing your own health or well-being for others. Attracting those who put excess demands on your time and energy. Feeling victimized or martyred by over-involvement in rescuing or healing others at your own expense.

———•———

Using psychological insight into the unconscious to manipulate others (especially when Pluto is involved.)

———•———

Encounters with deceit, lies, and secrets.

———•———

Nightmares and phobias (especially when Pluto is involved.)

———•———

Health issues:

Pisces rules the lymphatic system, immune system, fatty tissues and the feet in the physical body. The body/mind/spirit connection can bring on symptoms in these areas to signal the presence or stimulation of a Pisces or Twelfth House wound. Because of their resonance with the unconscious, the Twelfth House and the sign of Pisces are especially attuned to the body/mind/spirit connection, so hypochondria, psychosomatic conditions and stress-related symptoms and conditions can also present themselves.

PISCES
and/or the
TWELFTH
HOUSE

Pisces/Twelfth House continues...

STRATEGIES FOR HEALING

Spend time alone. This rejuvenates and restores, and is essential in order to connect with intuition and inner guidance, deepening your natural connection to Universal wisdom. Too much involvement with the outside world can be depleting. However, don't get so caught up in that inner world that you lose touch with what's going on everywhere else. Don't "drift away." Stay grounded by pulling yourself back regularly to the "real world" of day-to-day experiences and responsibilities.

———●———

Keep a dream journal.
What are they trying to tell you?

———●———

Make practices that integrate body, mind and spirit such as yoga and meditation part of your daily routine. Cultivate a healthy lifestyle.

———●———

Strengthen boundaries so you don't absorb others' negativity and pain. Your huge sensitivity can be draining if not protected.

———●———

Be on the alert for situations where you may be "giving yourself away" or following in another's path and losing your own direction in all relationships.

Use Pisces' visionary capabilities to see yourself whole and healed. Your lifestyle can then subtly align itself in ways that will manifest that vision.

———●———

Trust your innate intuition and your ability to recognize and read signs and symbols. Seek objective feedback from time to time to build certainty and confidence. Pisces and the Twelfth House can be confusing or unsettling at times. Sometimes a sore throat is simply a sore throat.

———●———

Accept necessary losses.
They are making space for growth and forward motion.

———●———

Act on your compassion by helping others in need without depleting yourself.

———●———

When Chiron is in the Twelfth House, finding a mentor who has dealt with similar challenges and or has the skills and abilities you are seeking to acquire yourself is particularly effective in the healing process. Then, pay it forward by becoming a mentor yourself.

PISCES
and/or the
TWELFTH
HOUSE

THE GOLD YOU'RE GOING FOR: ENERGIES/ABILITIES/SKILLS TO BE RELEASED

The courage to face the challenge and the power to heal the wound.

———●———

Superb abilities as therapists and healers of all kinds, especially in modalities addressing the body/mind/spirit connection.

———●———

Spiritual awareness. The ability to connect directly to Universal wisdom and the Divine.

———●———

Strong intuition and trust in its guidance.

———●———

The ability to recognize and read symbols, messages and dreams. Divination: reading the Tarot, runes, etc.

———●———

The ability to create a positive vision and manifest it through focused intent.

———●———

Sensitivity, compassion, and humility.

———●———

Creativity. Skills in photography and acting, especially.

———●———

The release of huge reservoirs of primal energy (especially when Pluto is involved.)

———●———

PISCES
and/or the
TWELFTH
HOUSE

APPENDIX

For the Record: Alice and Her Wounds
Astrology, Karma and You
Bibliography

FOR THE RECORD:
ALICE AND HER
WOUNDS

Pluto in Leo: Wounded Confidence and Self-Expression
Chiron in Cancer: Wounded Emotional Security

NTIL I IMMERSED MYSELF IN EVOLUTIONARY ASTROLOGY, I, LIKE SO many others, repeatedly encountered painful, limiting experiences without understanding their true source and significance, often wondering, "Why me?" Somehow, I'd soldier through, sometimes making a little progress and learning a little something. Sometimes not.

A particularly challenging life chapter opened up in my mid-thirties. I was living the full-out version of the "American Dream," at least as it had been defined by familial and societal expectations (which I had never thought to consider or question): the upwardly-mobile, college-sweetheart husband, two great kids, two dogs, two recent cars in the garage attached to the four-bedroom, three-bath house on an acre of land in the right suburb. "Good girl" that I was, I gave myself over to being the perfect wife and mother, never doubting that one stage of life would merge smoothly into the next, and that someday I'd see my girls continue the pattern into future generations. Until my husband left. (*Both wounds took a huge hit. Of course, the wounding itself had steered me right into this situation. I had rarely, if ever, had the sense of self or emotional confidence that would encourage me to design a life for myself, or to stand up for what I needed emotionally in relationships. Instead, I excelled at fulfilling others' expectations. Or so I had thought.)*

This was the late 70s/early 80s. Divorce and single parenthood as a societal norm were only vaguely on the radar, and in my square acre of suburban New Jersey, not on the scope at all. But I rallied. I didn't always get it right, but I tried my best and discovered I could pull off single parenting, without compromising my girls' connection to their father. (*The forced confrontation with the Chiron in Cancer wound released new, much-needed parenting skills.*) They've both turned out to be terrific, independent, accomplished, caring, long-time-married women, and I like to think I played a role in helping them achieve all that. I built a new career that I stayed with until the children were grown and I had attained the level in the corporate hierarchy that defined success for me. I mustered the moxie and left that secure career for astrology. (*Big-time progress on the Pluto in Leo wound.*) And, against all odds, I risked trust again and found Don. (*Emotional security reclaimed.*)

But there were definite bumps in the road along the way. Chief among them was a series of hospitalizations for hard-to-diagnose, elusive conditions that I later realized had their source in the body-mind connection. It had been hard-hit by the double whammy of emotional betrayal and self-depletion that resulted from juggling all those balls in the air without taking adequate care to replenish myself. (*Part of the Chiron in Cancer assignment is to nurture and care for yourself wisely and appropriately, and Chiron is the wound we're not motivated to heal.*)

In retrospect, I now see that at each milestone of this chapter of my life, encounters with my wounds released the energies needed for healing and for fueling forward motion in that life. Baby steps, giant steps. Forward and backwards. Just like in the childhood game of "May I?" They all count.

Pluto and Chiron, Both in the Tenth House:
Wounded Authority and the Ability to Achieve Goals

To quote myself earlier in these pages, this part of the birth chart represents "Life direction, goals and career; your 'mission.' Public persona and reputation; your effect on those who do not know you personally. The authoritarian parent (regardless of gender.) ...Pluto in the Tenth House provides exceptional power with the public and the opportunity to be influential and make positive contributions to one's society and culture."

I'd give myself a good score for taking on the role of the Authoritarian Parent. I also feel pretty solid on the career and mission dimension: I've found meaningful work that I love for many, many reasons. (The third try was the lucky charm...teaching French was very short-lived after college.) However, the part having to do with the public feels more like a B-. As I said in the Introduction, I know I can "take the show on the road," but I am always reluctant to do so. Professionally, I much prefer the one-on-one interaction with my clients and the solitude of writing. And I relish family and quiet personal time.

Some of the Tenth House themes resonate strongly with those associated with Cancer and Leo, the signs of my wounds, and because Pluto and Chiron are both in this house, the urgency of its healing mandate is more than doubled. With this third book, I've budgeted for some publicity and outreach. We'll see. Wish me well – as I do to you.

ASTROLOGY, KARMA AND YOU

YOU DON'T HAVE TO BELIEVE THAT WE INCARNATE MORE THAN ONCE TO benefit from what astrology can tell us about our life's possibilities, challenges, and potentials. I will be using the language of reincarnation, and I trust that if you've chosen to read this book, you'll at least be okay with that language and adapt it to your own needs. Just apply the information and explore the ideas in the context of a singular lifetime, if that's your perspective.

THE SPIRIT KNOWS

What did you come into this lifetime to experience, heal, and accomplish? How can you move towards those goals? What resources can you use? What challenges might you encounter? We are born with the answers to questions like these safely within us, but we need help unlocking them. Astrology is an important tool that can help us do just that. With this paragraph, we step through the doorway of evolutionary astrology, using it to gain understanding about how this lifetime fits into the overall journey of the growth of the spirit. The terrain we enter is for anyone interested in exploring the idea that life might hold meaning and purpose beyond that which is immediately perceptible in the physical, tangible world. And that our own spirit is a piece of that meaning and purpose.

We'll start with some core concepts.

KARMA

Simply stated, karma is the law of cause and effect. What we do now affects what happens later and what our options are. We incarnate to live the best, most meaningful life we can, and to move forward on the spiritual path. The ultimate goal is to "retire," to not have to reappear here on Earth because our spirit has learned what it needs to learn, contributed what it needs to contribute, and experienced what it needs to experience. In the language of reincarnation, we retire to Nirvana, which is a place "where the winds of karma do not blow." In Nirvana, the cosmic scales are in balance: all debts and obligations have been paid during our time here on Earth. All lessons have been learned and our spirit is back where it came from, reunited with the peace and beauty of the Universe's benevolence.

To help us reach our goals, the Universe provides experiences and opportunities that can help us learn and evolve. We make conscious choices, and those choices affect subsequent experiences, options, and decisions. And so on. If we choose the path of growth, which is likely to present some difficulties and challenges along the way, we can learn what we need to learn, close a spiritual gap, and move on to the next lesson. If we try to ignore the call of evolution and growth, the Universe may have to "up the ante" by delivering evermore dramatic and difficult challenges to get our attention. The choice of whether or not to grow in a positive direction is totally our own. We just have to be prepared to accept the consequences of our choices.

Where anyone else is on the path is simply not important. You only need to be conscious of where *you* are relative to where *you* are heading, and let everyone else do the same. This doesn't mean that you won't have mutually nurturing, inspiring relationships with other people, or not have opportunities to make a contribution to the world you live in. It's just that you're not in the business of comparing yourself to anyone but yourself when it comes to measuring progress. And you're not in the business of comparing yourself to some external standard of perfection, either. Your spirit knows where it's going and what it needs in order to get there. Although there are fellow travelers on the pilgrimage, the only standard for your progress is your own.

The good news is that you're more evolved than you've ever been. Now, here I'm on ground where there is some variety of opinion. I'm in the camp that believes we don't go backwards, even though sometimes it sure may feel like we do. Think of the wheels on a Conestoga wagon crossing the plains in a Western movie. The settlers are always heading toward the setting sun, but the camera and film speed are such that at times it looks like the wheels are rolling backwards. In other words, as cosmically "dumb" as we may sometimes feel, we were dumber in the karmic past.

REINCARNATION

It's not that difficult to build a case for the idea that you might have lived at some other time, in some other place, possibly even in another gender, race, or ethnicity. Think of Mozart writing sonatas from the age of six – or your own innate talents, for that matter. Where did they come from? Why doesn't anyone else in your family have them? We've all had experiences of *déjà vu*. And what about innate phobias? Why are some people terrified of lizards while others choose them for pets? There are psychological explanations for some of this, but they don't preclude a karmic one.

Underlying the concept of reincarnation is the idea that it would be hard for the spirit to learn everything it needs to know in order to retire to Nirvana after just one lifetime. Some lessons are complex and difficult, and all must be learned in the context of earthly life: providing for survival needs, engaging in meaningful relationships with others, fulfilling worldly responsibilities, having some fun.

The history of our lifetime's experiences and growth – the karmic equivalent of our high school "permanent record" – lies in something called the Akashic Records, karmic DNA, if you will. The Akashic Records are updated after each lifetime and the information stays with us no matter how many times we come back to this earthly plane. According to the perspective of evolutionary astrology, we are always being "promoted" to the next lifetime, even though there may be residual issues to be dealt with from the prior one(s). And no one is going to be reincarnated as a tarantula.

The karmic ledger is not always in perfect balance in one specific lifetime, but eventually it will be. In the tarot deck, there is a card called Justice that reflects this principle. It often shows up when we need a reminder that karmic justice *is* operating, even though it may not seem so in the day-to-day physical world. The keys that unlock the karmic carryover information are found in the symbols of each and every birth chart, along with the lesson plan for completing this lifetime's assignment.

BIBLIOGRAPHY

Braden, Greg. *Astrology and Spiritual Awakening.* Tempe. AZ: American Federation of Astrologers, 2014

Bogart, Greg. *The Divine Matrix: Bridging Time, Space, Miracles and Belief.* Carlsbad, CA: Hay House, 2007

Borysenko, Joan. *Fire in the Soul: A New Psychology of Spiritual Optimism.* New York, NY: Warner Books, 1993

Brooks, David. "Lady Gaga and the Life of Passion." New York, NY: *The New York Times,* October 23, 2015

Burt, Kathleen. *Archetypes of the Zodiac.* St. Paul, MN: Llewellyn Publications, 1988

Campbell, Joseph. *Pathways to Bliss: Mythology and Personal Transformation.* Novato, CA: New World Library, 2004

Caton, Gary R. "Saturn Opposite Uranus: Changing Times – and Minds." Cedar Ridge, CA: *The Mountain Astrologer,* June/July 2008

Clow, Barbara Hand. *Chiron: Rainbow Bridge Between the Inner and Outer Planets.* St. Paul, MN: Llewellyn Publications, 2001

Cooperman, Corrie. "Chiron Through the Houses." Cedar Ridge, CA: *The Mountain Astrologer,* August/September 2013

Cunningham, Donna. *Healing Pluto Problems.* York Beach, ME: Samuel Wiser, Inc., 1986

DeCastro, Dena. "Pluto Transits – Alchemy and Initiation." Cedar Ridge, CA: *The Mountain Astrologer,* February/March 2011

Finey, Michele. "The Chiron Return: The Journey Home." Cedar Ridge, CA: *The Mountain Astrologer,* April/May 2011

Fitzgerald, Hadley. "The Pluto Brothers Measure the Night." Cedar Ridge, CA: *The Mountain Astrologer,* December/January 2000-2001

Forrest, Jodie. "Pluto and the Norse Goddess Hel." Cedar Ridge, CA: *The Mountain Astrologer,* December 2001/January 2002

Forrest, Steven. *The Book of Pluto.* San Diego, CA: ACS Publications, 1994

Forrest, Steven. *The Faces of the Wound(CDs).* Lakeside, CA: Blue Sky Ranch, 2014

Greek Mythology.com

Green, Jeffrey. *Pluto: The Evolutionary Journey of the Soul.* St. Paul, MN: Llewellyn Publications, 1992

Greene, Liz. *The Astrology of Fate.* York Beach, ME: Samuel Wiser, Inc., 1984

Hand, Robert. *Planets in Transit.* West Chester, PA: Whitford Press, 1976

Hillenbrand, Candy. "The Centaur Connection: Expanding Chiron's Territory." Cedar Ridge, CA: *The Mountain Astrologer,* December 1999/January 2000

Howell, Alice O. *Jungian Symbolism in Astrology*. Wheaton, IL: The Theosophical Publishing House, 1987

Lesser, Elizabeth. *Broken Open. How Difficult Times Can Help Us Grow*. New York, NY: Villard Books (Random House), 2004

MacLaine, Shirley. *The Camino – A Journey of the Spirit*. New York, NY: Pocket Books (Simon and Schuster, Inc.), 2000

Michelsen, Neil F. *The American Ephemeris for the 20ᵗʰ Century*. San Diego, CA: ACS Publications, 1980, 1983, 1988

Michelsen, Neil F and Pottenger, Rique. *The American Ephemeris for the 21ˢᵗ Century 2000 to 2050*. San Diego, CA: ACS Publications, 1996

Murray, Jessica. "Saturn Without Suffering." Cedar Ridge, CA: *The Mountain Astrologer,* December 2016/January 2017

Nepo, Mark. *The Book of Awakening*. San Francisco, CA: Red Wheel/ Conari Press, 2000

New York Times.com (various)

Newton-John, Pierz. "Chiron: The Poison and the Medicine of Essence." Cedar Ridge, CA: *The Mountain Astrologer,* June/July 2000

Nolle, Richard. *Chiron – The New Planet in Your Horoscope*. Tempe, AZ: American Federation of Astrologers, 1997

Perry, Wendell C. "Pluto Generations." Cedar Ridge, CA: *The Mountain Astrologer,* February/March 2015

Reinhart, Melanie. *Chiron and the Healing Journey*. London, England: Penguin Books, 1998

Tyl, Noel, editor. *How to Personalize the Outer Planets*. St. Paul, MN: Llewellyn Publications, 1992 : Green, Jeffrey. "Trauma and the Outer Planets." ; Jawer, Jeff. ; "The Outer Planets and the Inner Spirit." ; Shea, Mary E. "Making Choices with Outer Planet

Transits." ; Wickenburg, Joanne. "Bringing the Outer Planets Down to Earth."

Wikipedia.org (various)

Younghans, Pam. "Chiron: Healing the Child-Self." Cedar Ridge, CA: *The Mountain Astrologer,* February/March 2016

AUTHOR PROFILE

ALICE LOFFREDO

IN 1993 ALICE LOFFREDO LEFT A SUCCESSFUL CAREER AS A SYSTEMS manager for a major insurance company to follow the calling of her own birth chart and start an astrological consulting practice. She has taught astrology and tarot for private students and the local community college, and is a popular lecturer at workshops, special interest groups, charity events, and bookstores. The first book of what she knew from the start would be a karmic trilogy, *Perfect Together: Astrology, Karma and You*, was published in 2008. *Your Astrological Compass* followed in 2013. *Healing the Karmic Wounds* completes the trifecta. She lives in central New Jersey with her husband Don and Dolly, the best rescue-cat ever.

You can learn more about Alice and her work by visiting www.AstrologyKarmaAndYou.com

CPSIA information can be obtained
at www.ICGtesting.com
Printed in the USA
FFHW01n1415220818
47808590-51529FF